# COLLEGE LIBRARY NEWSLETTERS

## CLIP Note # 13

*Compiled by*

**Patricia Smith Butcher**
*Assistant Director of Readers' Services*
*Roscoe L. West Library*
*Trenton State College*
*Trenton, New Jersey*

**Susan McCarthy Campbell**
*Library Director*
*Schmidt Library*
*York College of Pennsylvania*
*York, Pennsylvania*

D0022352

College Library Information Packet Committee
College Libraries Section
Association of College and Research Libraries
A Division of the American Library Association

ASSOCIATION OF
COLLEGE
& RESEARCH
LIBRARIES

Published by the Association of College and Research Libraries
A Division of the American Library Association
50 East Huron Street
Chicago, IL 60611-2795
312-280-2515
Toll-free 1-800-545-2433 ext. 2515

ISBN: 0-8389-7445-7

The paper used in this publication meets the minimum requirements of American
National Standard for Information Sciences—Permanence of Paper for Printed
Library Materials, ANSI Z39.48-1984. ∞

# TABLE OF CONTENTS

i

# CLIP NOTES COMMITTEE

Jonathan D. Lauer, Chair
Messiah College

Dan Bedsole
Randolph Macon College

James Cubit
Williams College

Ray English
Oberlin College

Victoria Hanawalt
Reed College

Pamela Snelson
Drew University

# INTRODUCTION

**Objective:**

The College Library Information Packet Notes publishing program, under the auspices of the College Libraries Section of the Association of College and Research Libraries, provides "college and small university libraries with state-of-the-art reviews and current documentation on library practices and procedures of relevance to them." (Morein, 226) This CLIP Note offers information and ideas about the development, design, and production of the college library newsletter.

**Background:**

The newsletter is a thriving form of promotion and communication. It can be a fast, effective, and economical device to foster public awareness about services, staff and programs, provide visibility, and communicate with readers.

Although the professional literature contains little information about the production of a library newsletter, a number of college libraries are utilizing the newsletter as a component of their communications and public relations programs. While each is as unique as the institution which produced it, college library newsletters share basic start up questions focusing on purpose, cost, layout, audience, staffing, distribution, and quality control. Producing a college library newsletter requires varying degrees of thought, planning, time and money. One veteran newsletter editor sagely advised "Before throwing your hat into the arena of newsletter publishers, it is important that you know what you are getting into and be sure you want to do it." (Ford, 682) This CLIP Note explores the basics of college library newsletter development and production. It provides examples to assist college libraries in producing newsletters that can be valuable sources of information and useful public relations tools.

**Survey Procedure:**

The procedure followed was the standard one for CLIP Note projects. The CLIP Note Committee of ACRL's College Libraries Section reviewed a proposal and drafts of a questionnaire. In November 1989, 256 small and medium-sized academic libraries received the revised questionnaire. The mailing list consisted of libraries classified by the Carnegie Council on Policy Studies in Higher Education (1976) as either Comprehensive University and College I or Liberal Arts Colleges I. All libraries had previously agreed to participate in CLIP Note surveys. In addition to completing the questionnaire, those libraries with newsletters returned copies of their newsletters and style manuals or policy guidelines.

**Survey Results:**

A total of 168 of the 256 questionnaires were returned for a 65.6 percent response rate. Fifty-three (31.5 percent) of the libraries in the sample publish a newsletter. The tabulated questionnaire with complete summaries of responses is included.

Using the most frequently cited responses, a sketch of the typical college library newsletter emerges. It is produced primarily for publicity and promotion of library services for faculty, staff, and administration. A permanent editor, usually the library director, is responsible for publishing irregular or occasional issues. A campus printing facility produces 150-300 copies of each issue. In the one to five years the library has been producing a newsletter, staff time is the main problem. Contributors are overwhelmingly

1

library staff. In addition to text, in-house graphics are used. Staff profiles are a regular feature. The newsletter is one to four pages long. It is not produced with desktop software, but probably will be soon. It is distributed through campus mail and costs up to $500 annually, not including staff time. No style manual is used. There are usually one to five responses to articles in each issue. The feedback is verbal and highly positive. Samples submitted would indicate further that the typical newsletter is 8 1/2 by 11 inches, stapled in the upper left hand corner, and is either white or buff colored.

A closer examination of completed questionnaires and samples reveals a broad range of possibilities for producing a library newsletter. For complete details, see the tabulated questionnaire.

## Goals of Library Newsletters (Questions 3 and 4)

Publicity or promotion is the major goal of producing a newsletter for 51 of the 53 respondents. The question should have included communicating information as a possible response, as 15 respondents indicate that this is their goal. Only seven libraries use the newsletters as a means to attract donors.

The primary audience of all 53 newsletters includes faculty, administration, and staff. Nearly half, 26, are published for students also. Other audiences are friends groups, alumni, other libraries, retirees, and boards of trustees.

## Content (Questions 5-6, 12-14, and 19)

A permanent editor is responsible for the content of 35 of the 53 newsletters. Sixteen of the 35 permanent editors are library directors. Ten newsletters have rotating editors, while eight are governed by an editorial board or committee. Professional librarians hold the editorial position(s) of 48 newsletters, while staff have these positions on nine publications. Library staff contribute articles to all 53 newsletters. Faculty outside the library write articles for eight of them. Students, friends, computer center staff, and the college president contribute to others.

The newsletters are primarily text. However, 32 contain graphics, nine have photographs, and 12 have illustrations. Twenty-seven respondents produce non-textual material in house, 22 use clip art, while four employ professional art work. Additional responses include wood engravings and computer graphics.

Staff profiles are the most frequently cited regular feature, appearing in 26 of the newsletters. In addition, 23 contain collection profiles, 18 include reviews, and 15 feature regular columns. The columns typically consist of departmental news.

Only three of the respondents have a style manual or written policy guidelines for the newsletter. Two additional editors note a personal preference for Turabian or MLA style guides.

## Production, Distribution (Questions 7-10, 15-18)

Library newsletters are not usually tied to a regular publication schedule. The most common response is irregular or occasional, while the range is one to eight issues annually. Almost half of the respondents print 150-300 copies an issue. Only three libraries print over a thousand copies. A campus printing facility prints 32 of the newsletters. Fourteen are printed in the library, while seven are printed commercially. The majority of the libraries (30) have produced a newsletter for one to five years. Four newsletters have been publishing less than a year, and only seven are older than ten years.

Most of the newsletters (35) are one to four pages long, while 14 are five to ten pages. Few are longer than ten, although one respondent indicates 25 pages.

Desktop publishing is used for 24 newsletters. Word Perfect is the most frequently used software. Many of the 29 editors who do not use a software program indicate a desire to do so.

Campus mail is the primary means of distribution for newsletters, used by 49 libraries. Newsletters are sent by U.S. mail by 15 libraries and put out for pick up or as handouts in 18 libraries.

Most respondents (38) indicate an annual cost of $0-500. Only three have an annual newsletter budget in excess of $1000. These costs do not include staff time.

### Problems, Reactions (Questions 11 and 20)

Staff time is cited by 45 of 52 respondents as a main problem in producing a newsletter. Cost, lack of response from the intended audience, and difficulties with soliciting interesting articles and illustrations are much less frequently problematic.

Library newsletters generally do not generate a large number of responses. While 42 of the respondents indicate receiving responses from readers, only ten receive more than five per issue. All 42 indicate receiving verbal responses, while 24 indicate receiving written responses. Responses are largely positive (38). Only eight respondents receive negative feedback, but no one mentions specific criticisms.

### Libraries without Newsletters (Question 2)

Those 115 responding libraries without newsletters use a wide variety of methods to communicate information. Most contribute articles to other campus publications, e.g., 84 to the student newspaper and 76 to the campus staff/faculty/administration newsletter. Memoranda, notices, and special mailings are employed by 28 respondents. Friends newsletters are published by 14 libraries.

### Selection of Documents

The complete newsletters reproduced in this CLIP Note illustrate a variety of production methods, those produced on campus, in the library or commercially. Nameplate and graphic examples are included. Also highlighted are style manuals and guidelines for guest editors.

# REFERENCES

Ford, Sylverna. "The Library Newsletter: Is It For You?" College and Research Libraries News 49 (1988):678-682.

Morein, P. Grady. "What is a CLIP Note?" College and Research Libraries News 46 (1985):226-229.

Snelson, Pamela. "Ten Years of CLIPpings." CLS Newsletter 5 (1989-90):1-3.

"Starting Your Own Newsletter." Changing Times 40 (April, 1986):77-80.

# CLIP Note Survey
# Library Newsletters
# Results

Institution name _____

_____ public

_____ private

Address _____

_____

_____

Name of respondent _____

Title _____

_____ Check here if this is an address or name change.

Telephone Number _____

*Number of F.T.E. students   156 responses; Range 560-5000; Mean 1755.3; Median 1588*

For each question, please check all answers that apply to your library's newsletter.

1.  Do you publish a library newsletter as a means of communicating information about services and collections to the college community? (Please note. This CLIP Note will not include staff newsletters.)

    *168 responses*

    __53__ Yes.  Proceed to question 3.
    __115__ No.   Proceed to question 2 and return the questionnaire.
               Thank you.

2.  If you do not publish a newsletter, do you                *111 responses*

    __84__ contribute articles to the student newspaper?
    __76__ contribute articles to a staff/faculty/administration newsletter?
    __14__ publish a Friends newsletter?
    __69__ use other means of communication?

Please explain.

| | |
|---|---|
| memoranda, notices, special mailings | 28 |
| accession or acquisitions lists | 14 |
| announcements at meetings | 11 |
| alumni publication | 8 |
| campus newspaper or magazine | 5 |
| handouts or brochures | 4 |
| library committee | 3 |
| other committees | 2 |
| computing center newsletter | 2 |
| departmental newsletter (documents, media) | 2 |
| bulletin boards, posters, signs | 2 |
| local newspaper | 2 |
| college schedule | 2 |
| face to face, walking around talking | 2 |
| bibliographic notes | 1 |
| ads in student newspaper | 1 |
| library workshops | 1 |
| consortia newsletter | 1 |
| affiliated church newsletter | 1 |
| campus computer network | 1 |
| library student handbook | 1 |
| monthly information table | 1 |
| student newsletter | 1 |
| work study newsletter | 1 |
| other vehicles on campus | 1 |
| sponsor special events (poetry readings) | 1 |
| student radio station | 1 |
| annual report | 1 |
| internal library report | 1 |

3.  What is/are the major goal(s) of producing the newsletter?   *53 responses*

   _51_  Publicity/promotion
   _7_   Attract donors
   _18_  Other
         Please explain.

| | |
|---|---|
| information or communication | 15 |
| educational tool | 1 |
| library hours schedule | 1 |
| acquisitions list | 1 |

4.  For whom is your newsletter published?   *53 responses*

   _53_  Faculty, staff, administration
   _26_  Students
   _4_   Alumni
   _13_  Friends
   _10_  Other
         Please explain.

| | |
|---|---|
| other libraries | 5 |
| consortium members | 4 |
| library retirees | 2 |
| emeritus faculty and administrators | 1 |
| board of trustees | 1 |
| any registered user who requests subscription | 1 |

5. Who is responsible for your library's newsletter? *53 responses*

| 35 | Permanent editor | |
| | Position of permanent editor | |
| | Director | 16 |
| | Reference Librarian | 4 |
| | Director's Secretary | 2 |
| | Special Services Librarian | 1 |
| | Government Documents Librarian | 1 |
| | Public Services Librarian | 1 |
| 10 | Rotating Editor | |
| 8 | Editorial Board or Committee | |
| | Director and Secretary | 1 |
| | Director and Reference Coordinator | 1 |
| | Reference and BI Librarian and Director of Media Resources Center | 1 |
| | Head of Circulation and Information and Computing Services and Coordinator of User Services | 1 |

6. Is the editor or board *53 responses*

| 48 | professional librarian(s)? |
| 9 | staff member(s)? |
| 2 | other? |
| | Please explain. |

| professional administrator | 1 |
| academic computer center staff member and library director | 1 |

7. How frequently is your newsletter published? *53 responses*

| | Weekly |
| | Bi-weekly |
| | Twice monthly |
| 5 | Monthly |
| 48 | Other |
| | Please explain. |

| irregularly or occasionally | 11 |
| quarterly | 9 |
| one per semester | 6 |
| two-four per semester | 5 |
| bi-annually | 3 |
| two-four per year | 6 |
| bi-monthly | 2 |
| five per year | 2 |
| six per year | 2 |
| seven per year | 1 |
| annually | 1 |

8. How many copies are printed? *53 responses*

| 11 | 0 - 150 |
| 24 | 150 - 300 |
| 9 | 300 - 500 |
| 7 | 500 - 1000 |
| 3 | Over 1000 |

Note: One library indicates printing different numbers of copies as needed.

9.     Where is your newsletter printed?          *53 responses*

      15     In the library
      32     In a campus printing facility
      7     By a commercial printer
           Other
           Please specify.

           Note: Two of the 53 respondents indicate using a combination of two methods of printing.

10.    How long have you produced a newsletter?       *53 responses*

      4     Less than a year
      30     1 - 5 years
      12     6 - 10 years
      7     More than 10 years

11.    What are the main problems with producing a newsletter?    *52 responses*

      5     Cost
      45     Staff time
      7     Lack of response from intended audience
      5     Other
           Please explain.

| | |
|---|---|
| getting enough articles written | 1 |
| obtaining illustrations | 1 |
| concocting interesting articles | 1 |
| lack of knowledge of desktop publishing | 1 |
| no problems | 1 |

12.    Who contributes to the newsletter?         *53 responses*

      53     Library staff
      8     Faculty
      1     Students
      4     Others
           Please explain.

| | |
|---|---|
| computer center staff | 2 |
| college president | 1 |
| friends officers | 1 |

13.    Does your newsletter contain         *53 responses*

      32     graphics?
      9     photographs?
      12     other illustrations?
           Please explain how these are done.
               27   in-house
               4   professional
               22   clip art
               Additional responses

| | |
|---|---|
| wood engravings | 1 |
| computer | 1 |

14. In addition to news and features, does your newsletter regularly include
*37 responses*

  15   columns?
       Please list.

| | |
|---|---|
| director, department heads | 8 |
| gifts | 3 |
| who's reading what | 3 |
| acquisitions or accessions | 2 |
| staff activities | 2 |
| special collections and archives | 2 |
| friends | 2 |
| automation | 2 |
| typical reference questions | 1 |
| puzzle | 1 |
| DIALOG | 1 |
| cost,purchase,selection of undergraduate materials | 1 |

  18   reviews?
  26   staff profiles?
  23   collection profiles?
   6   other?
       Please explain.

| | |
|---|---|
| current interest news, bibliographies | 3 |
| editorials | 1 |
| thematic quotations | 1 |
| new professional staff | 1 |
| professional achievements | 1 |
| non-traditional services | 1 |

15. How many pages is your newsletter?
*52 responses*

  35   1 - 4
  14   5 - 10
   2   More than 10
   4   Other
       Please explain.

| | |
|---|---|
| 4 or 6 | 1 |
| 8 - 16 | 1 |
| depends on amount and length of worthy articles | 1 |
| combined with booklist, sometimes 25 pages | 1 |

16. Do you use desktop publishing software?
*53 responses*

  24   Yes.
       If so, what program?

| | |
|---|---|
| Word Perfect | 5 |
| First Publisher | 3 |
| Pagemaker | 4 |
| Newsroom | 2 |
| Display Write | 1 |
| Graphic Writer | 1 |
| Mac Write | 2 |
| Microsoft Word | 1 |
| Newsmaster | 1 |
| Smart | 1 |
| Superpaint | 1 |
| VAX word processing | 1 |
| Wordstar | 1 |

  29   No

17. How is your newsletter distributed? *53 responses*

   _49_ Campus mail
   _15_ U.S. mail
   _18_ Pick up or handout

18. What is the estimated annual cost of producing your newsletter? (Not including staff time.) *51 responses*

   _38_ $ 0 - 500
   _5_ $500 - 1000
   _3_ over $1000
   _5_ not known

19. Do you have a written style manual or policy guidelines for your newsletter? *53 responses*

   _3_ Yes.
   _50_ No.

       Note: Two respondents answer no, but indicate using Turabian and MLA.

20. Do you receive responses to articles appearing in your newsletter? *52 responses*

   _42_ Yes
       If so, are they

       _24_ Written
       _42_ Verbal
       _38_ Positive
       _8_ Negative

       Please estimate how frequently you receive responses (number per issue).

| | |
|---|---|
| 1 - 5 | 19 |
| 5 - 12 | 6 |
| 10 -15 | 2 |
| less than 20 | 2 |
| erratic | 1 |

   _10_ No.

# Campus Produced Newsletters

# *Contents*

## Ellen Clarke Bertrand Library
## Bucknell University

Format: folder

Size: 8 1/2 by 11"

Color: green

Number of pages: 4

Frequency: quarterly

Annual cost: $500 - 1,000

Number of copies: 500 - 1,000

Audience: faculty, staff, administration, friends, library consortia, board of trustees

Editorial responsibility: rotating editor; professional librarian or administrator

Desktop software: Pagemaker

BERTRAND LIBRARY, BUCKNELL UNIVERSITY

# CONTENTS

**Volume V, No. 1**

**Fall 1989**

A Newsletter of the Ellen Clarke Bertrand Library

## Digging for Irish Treasure
### by Susan Swartzlander

This summer I led my English 381 students on an expedition to the Emerald Isle. We landed not in Dublin or Shannon, but in the Bertrand Library's special collections whose extensive holdings of Irish materials include the correspondence of Oliver St. John Gogarty, George Bernard Shaw, Lord Dunsany, George Russell, Augustus John, and William Butler Yeats.

I still feel an exhilaration when I hold a faded Yeats letter with a scrawl that communicates something palpable about the spirit of the poet. Because I wanted my students to experience this *manuscript mystique* too, the final project for English 381 was an edition of a letter from special collections. Early in the semester, the students attended an orientation session given by reference librarian Nancy Weyant and special collections/archives specialist Doris Dysinger, during which they learned about the fundamentals of handling manuscripts, from how to touch them to how to request permission for their publication.

After choosing letters that captured their interests, the students started the detective work of identifying names, dates, places, and events mentioned in their letters. Where statements in the correspondence were puzzling, students turned to other letters for clarification. Attempting to place their letters in biographical, literary, historical, and political contexts, the students read voraciously about Ireland, as well as about their correspondents. The letters the students chose determined the direction their reading took.

Les Mohapp edited a September 5, 1941 letter from Oliver St. John Gogarty to Mary Owens Miller which captured the spirit of the Yeats-Gogarty friendship. Alex Gruenberg found a January 22, 1921 letter from Gogarty to Seymour Leslie, cousin of Winston Churchill, that illustrates just how untidy

(see **Treasure**, page 4)

*Ballylee -- Yeats' Tower Home*

## EDUCOM Meeting
### by Ann de Klerk

*Ann de Klerk and JoAnne Young attended the 25th anniversary EDUCOM conference at Ann Arbor, Michigan, October 16 through 19, 1989.*

What is EDUCOM? EDUCOM is a non-profit consortium of 590 colleges and universities concerned with computing and communications issues. EDUCOM programs focus on networking, integrating computing into the curriculum, and information access and dissemination. Attendees included faculty, university administrators, and information professionals.

A highlight of all EDUCOM conferences are the demonstrations by the Corporate Associates, including the giants IBM, Apple, NEXT, and others. Of great interest to us was the Software Showcase, allowing hands-on experience with almost 100 courseware products, many developed by faculty at member institutions.

EDUCOM is always thought-provoking and invigorating, inspiring us with new ideas of how to continue to build upon information access initiatives within the Bertrand Library.

CONTENTS/PAGE 2

## A Fresh Approach
### by Roberta Laulicht Sims

This September the Ellen Clarke Bertrand Library adopted a new approach to Freshmen Orientation activities. Although exposure to the physical layout of the library remains important, the focus this year was on introducing incoming students to Bucknell librarians and staff members.

Traditionally Freshman Orientation in the Bertrand Library has consisted of a tour of the building and a reception for students and their families. This year, the Bertrand Library added "round robin" techniques which involved professional librarians giving brief presentations to various services and sources of information available at the Bertrand Library.

New tours began every fifteen minutes. This staggered approach to tours allowed for small groups, and provided a personalized environment. A tour guide led the group through the building, stopping at four key points along the way, where they were given short, introductory sessions to important resources.

Zoya Jenks, catalog librarian, and Jim Van Fleet, reference librarian, demonstrated the library's online catalog system. Another stopping point, the ABI/INFORM station (which provides full text from business periodicals), introduced the students to reference librarian Debora Cheney, who demonstrated this vital new CD-ROM source. In the Reference Area, tour groups were met by reference librarians Nancy Weyant or Diane Kovacs for an overview of the layout of available reference services and sources. On the second floor, in the Periodicals Area, head catalog librarian Paul Boytinck or collection development librarian George Jenks acquainted the groups with the library's collection of periodicals and newspapers.

A refreshment table, located in the after hours study area, allowed students and parents to view the MacIntosh computer lab, the 24-hour study area, and the vending lounge.

Positive feedback from parents, students, and librarians indicate that the "round robin" approach to orientation may become the tradition of the future.

## Listening/Viewing Room

The Bertrand Library now has a listening/viewing room equipped with a TV and VCR, plus a variety of sound-recording playback equipment. The listening/viewing room, located on level two, room 209, is available to all students, faculty, and staff during regular library hours.

## Coming Spring Semester: Keyword Online Searching
### by Debora Cheney

Nearly a year has passed since we first made the Online Catalog available to the Bucknell University community. During the year we have introduced students and faculty to the Online Catalog and have been gratified by their ready acceptance of this new format for an old research tool. Now, additional improvements are on the way. When the students return for spring semester, the Bertrand Library staff will be ready to introduce them to keyword searching in the Online Catalog.

Keyword searching will provide additional flexibility beyond what is currently available by allowing library users to look for works available in Bertrand Library whose titles or subject headings contain specific "keywords," or "keyword phrases." Keyword access will allow the user to search for these key words without knowing the exact order of those words in the titles or subject headings. Keyword searching will allow the library user to look for works available in Bertrand Library containing different combinations of keywords and keyword phrases. This flexibility is especially useful to the researcher or student who is trying to locate all the materials available on a specific subject.

Keyword access to the Online Catalog will provide Bucknell University community with a state-of-the-art research tool. As information becomes more important in our information-based society, so too are the tools we use to access that information. At Bertrand Library we are working to ensure that the Bucknell University community has these new tools at their fingertips.

*Reference librarian / user education coordinator Dot Thompson and associate professor of religion Joe La Barge recently attended a workshop together conducted by Evan Farber, a nationally recognized leader in course-intergrated library instruction featured in the last issue of CONTENTS. In this issue we hear the individual responses from this faculty / librarian team.*

## Guru of Library Instruction
### by Dot Thompson

After reading so much about Evan Farber's Bibliographic Instruction program at Earlham College, I was eager to hear the guru of library instruction speak. As he discussed the problems observed at Earlham, the solutions to those problems, and the role of an effective user education program, it was clear that Bucknell shared his concerns.

Most reference librarians would agree with Farber's description of the panicky, insecure feeling many students have in a college library. Library instruction should counter any negative feelings; with instruction at all stages of the educational career the student's information skills should grow as his or her needs grow.

Another problem Farber addressed was the difficulty students often encounter with their assignments. Assignments are often inadequately stated or create unrealistic goals which inadvertently encourage students to avoid the library. This happens at Bucknell also. Sometimes we have wild nights at the Reference Desk with every third student coming to us for help on the same assignment with only a vague idea of where to start. Often we see students change their topic when they do not immediately find something on their first idea.

Farber has another concern that most of us share: the general failure of students to evaluate and be critical about the sources they cite. Students need to learn to read the titles looking for clues to the content of the article. They need to be learning the experts in their field. Librarians can encourage and foster critical thinking by providing students with some information skills to equip them with the confidence to evaluate and question what they read.

At Bucknell, as at Earlham, we are developing a results-oriented library instruction program. Short term results of an effective user education program are high quality work drawn from sophisticated sources. Long range results are the creation of independent learners and students who feel like "junior faculty" and "junior researchers." Students who graduate feeling comfor-

able in a library, who can approach a library with confidence and a sence of empowerment, those students are on their way to becoming professionals.

## Working the Library
### by Joseph A. La Barge

By now the symptoms have become familiar. You assign a research paper, give your students some general instructions, maybe even devote a special class to "bibliographic research," turn them loose in the library and then wait. The results? A few truly impressive projects, many mediocre works and some so poorly developed that it hurts to read them. What's the problem? Ideas only partially developed; significant information and data missing; few sources consulted; opinions strung together like popcorn on a string. Is it poor writing? Sometimes, but you also know at least some of these same students are decent writers. Is there a deeper problem? Yes, and I believe it's called "The Library." That labyrinth of endless stacks, that maze of computer screens, that place were so many (even upperclass) students confess to feeling anxious, helpless, and out of control.

> "While the two groups -- teaching faculty and librarians -- can and should work together, neither one can do the other's job."
> **Evan Farber**

With these thoughts in mind I was particularly eager to hear Evan Farber, head librarian at Earlham College, speak at Susquehanna University on September 16, 1989. What Farber said confirmed ideas I had been trying to clarify for several years: if the library is to effectively enhance the teaching-learning process, we (faculty and students) will need to change the way we understand it and use it. Specifically, we need to design more realistic library assignments, introduce our students to the library's resources earlier and more gradually in our courses and work closely in all this with our reference librarians.

This need not be an impossible task. Bucknell's library staff is eager to help, full of good ideas, and willing to share examples of successful projects from colleagues in a wide variety of disciplines. Sounds like a project worth exploring over a January, part of a summer, or while on sabbatical.

CONTENTS/PAGE 4

## Yolla Bolly Press at Fifteen
### by Roberta Laulicht Sims

The Bertrand Library is pleased to be exhibiting the fine book art of the Yolla Bolly Press. The exhibit will include woodblocks, broadsides, ephemera, and limited edition books representing the accomplishments of the Yolla Bolly Press over the past fifteen years.

Carolyn and James Robertson, owners of The Yolly Bolly Press, began making books in 1975. Their studio, a redwood barn, is located in the rural town of Covelo, California. They produce books not only for major companies, but they also create handmade limited edition publications. A four volume series, *California Writers of the Land*, included Robinson Jeffers' prose poem *Cawdor* (1983); John Steinbeck's *Flight* (1984); *The Daring Young Man on the Flying Trapeze and Other Stories* by William Saroyan (1984), and *True Bear Stories*, by Joaquin Miller (1985). Other fine editions include *My First Summer in the Sierra*, by John Muir, and *The Inland Whale* by Theodora Kroeber.

As a way of passing on their knowledge about design and printing, the Robertsons maintain an active apprenticeship program at The Yolla Bolly Press. Currently, two Bucknell graduates are working as assistants for the Robertsons: Nancy Campbell, '85, and Doug Anderson, '84.

"Yolla Bolly Press At Fifteen" will be on display in the Bertrand Library from January 2 through April 13, 1990, on Lower Level One.

## Treasure (continued from page 1)

Irish history can be. Bettina Jaeger chose a January 6, 1931 (or 1932) letter from George Yeats (William Butler Yeats' wife) to Gogarty which warns Gogarty that should he decide to rent Ballylee, the Yeats tower home, he should not expect an Irish Hilton. The fourth student, Wendy Weibel, chose a December 1937 letter from Augustus John, the Irish painter, to Oliver St. John Gogarty. Her essay focused particularly on John's request for Gogarty's help in preventing a committee from showing one of his paintings at the Louvre.

Thanks to Bertrand Library's staff, my English 381 students gained more than specific knowledge about elegies on William Butler Yeats, or the Black and Tans, or medieval towers, or Irish portrait painting. They learned not only about a culture and particular personalities of the Irish renaissance, but also about scholarship. They have a new appreciation for the demands of biographical and textual work. They learned not only about what scholars do, but why we do it -- they have experienced first-hand the *manuscript mystique*.

**Editor:** Roberta Laulicht Sims

*CONTENTS* is published quarterly by the Ellen Clarke Bertrand Library, Bucknell University, Lewisburg, PA 17837. Comments, inquiries and letters should be addressed to the editor.

# BUCKNELL

**Ellen Clarke Bertrand Library**
**Bucknell University**
**Lewisburg, PA 17837**

# *Butler University Library News*

## Irwin Library System
## Butler University

Format: stapled

Size: 8 1/2 by 11"

Color: white

Number of pages: 5 - 10

Frequency: bi-annually

Annual cost: $0 - 500

Number of copies: 150 - 300

Audience: faculty, staff, administration, and friends

Editorial responsibility: permanent editor; reference librarian

Desktop software: Word Perfect 5.0

# BUTLER UNIVERSITY
# LIBRARY NEWS

## An Irwin Library System Publication

**FALL 1989**

### ELECTRONIC LIBRARY

Harvard and Yale have it. Soon Butler will also. It is library automation, part of the campus-wide "Butler Connection" project. A $1.5 million gift from Ruth Lilly will be used largely toward automating the library. Librarians have been working closely with the Computer Center to select an optimal system and the Data Research Associates Atlas System has been chosen.

For faculty at their office computers the **system will provide subject, author and title access to the holdings of the Butler libraries** as well as to CD-ROM products such as ERIC, Psychlit, ABI Inform, etc. Additional CD's such as the Oxford English Dictionary and Academic American Encyclopedia could be added. In addition to bibliographic sources, some full text sources will be available. Specialized databases utilizing selected collections here at Butler may be developed. It will be possible to download on to a personal computer from any of these sources or from an online database and then to manipulate the data or print it as necessary. **A professor sitting in an office will be able to create personalized bibliographies.** These wonders will not occur all at one time. The goal is to have phase one of the system operating by September, 1990.

We invite suggestions for a name and acronym to describe our system. BULLDOG for Butler University Library Linkage Data Online Genie has been suggested, but we suspect that improvements are possible. Use terms like: automated, database, information system, research and bibliographies. Please send your suggestions to John Kondelik, Director of Libraries. If your acronym is chosen, you will be made an honory Friend of the Irwin Library.

### FRIENDS OF THE IRWIN LIBRARY

We appreciate our Friends and want more! Our first invitation to membership yielded fifty-six members, some of whom met for a pleasant evening recently to view a film, hear a talk by Gisela Terrell, Rare Books and Special Collections Librarian, about preserving our collections, and to socialize. If you are one of those who almost joined but buried the form under a stack of papers, please reconsider. A call to 283-9226 will speed the information to you.

### FACULTY RESEARCH SHARING

Have you heard a colleague discussing her research and wished you could read it without having to wait for it to be published? Have you wished for comments on your work from that professor in another discipline who might happen to know something you don't know he knows?

**Faculty work in process** may now be placed oh reserve at Irwin, Science, and Fine Arts Libraries where it will be available for review by colleagues and if desired, by students. This idea surfaced at the November Faculty Forum on "The Role of Research at Butler. University". In response to the keynote speech by author John Lukacs, **President Bannister** made the point that research need not have been published to be valuable, that the process itself is of great value and that the stimulation of sharing ones ideas as they evolve can not only enhance scholarship but can stimulate others in their endeavors.

A librarian in attendance suggested that the library would be the logical place to facilitate and nurture the sharing of manuscripts. We have now worked out the details. Simply deliver three copies of your work to whichever library you request. We will distribute the copies to each library to encourage interdisciplinary communioations. If you do not want marks on your manuscript, it would be a good idea to include a note to that effect and a few sheets of blank paper for comments. Watch this bi-annual newsletter and also library bulletin boards for lists of work available for perusal. Your suggestions about this plan are as welcome as your manuscripts.

It is possible to copyright a draft. Forms for copyright registration will soon be available in the Irwin Library Reference Department. At some universities it is standard procedure to secure registration of copyright prior to circulating work among colleagues.

Published work may also be placed on reserve for perusal and/or comment. If you do not have your journal article, give us the citation and we will obtain a copy of it. Many books by faculty are already catalogued in library collections. We do make an effort to obtain all faculty books, so if we have missed yours, please let us know.

Archives contain many faculty papers, particularly those resulting from sabbatical leaves, grants and fellowships. The Fine Arts Library preserves faculty compositions.

**THE PATRICIA MESZAROS COLLECTION**

The library collection has been enriched by the acquisition of many volumes on 17th and 18th century literature which came from the personal library of our former Dean of Liberal Arts and Science. Her fine library filled many gaps in our collections.

**LIBRARY PEOPLE**

We welcome Shelley Lesandrini to the Cataloging Department - she assists in Reference, also. We celebrate the return of Jean Cauger-Chipper to Acquisitions. Sharon Lewis has moved from Reference to head a new department, Information Access and Document Delivery. Nancy Everett has been promoted to Head of Collection Management where whe is working industriously while her predecessor, Vera Schornhorst, enjoys retirement. Vera is one of the charter members of the Friends of the Library.

**THE WINNER**

Director Kondelik has won for us a one year subscription to the **Monthly Catalog** of the Government Printing Office on CD. The CD covers from July 1976 to the present and is updated bi-monthly. Now instead of looking through 80 volumes, you look at one monitor in the reference room at Irwin. At least for the present we will have improved access to our government documents collection.

CD ROM products are appearing in increasing numbers in many disciplines and are greatly expanding library capability to assist in thorough as well as speedy bibliographic research. In an article in Academe ("The Electronic Library and the Challenge of Information Planning," July-August 1989, p12) Timothy Weiskel discusses the problems of paying for CD's and suggests that "departments and research institutes could be fully informed of the CD Rom's general utility and asked to contribute to its costs in the library." Cooperation of this nature already is practiced between the College of Business and Irwin Reference.

## IN THE PUBLIC EYE

Irwin Library is featured in an ad which appeared recently in American Libraries and Library Journal. University Microfilms, Inc., from whom we acquired most of our microfilm collection and assistance with our microfilm room, has served an important role in the library's plan for serials management. The ad recounts the serious deficiencies in periodicals six years ago when John Kondelik became Director and shows how UMI assisted the library in raising its success rate in supplying patrons with periodicals to 75/80 percent.

## BOTH BORROWER AND LENDER

Interlibrary loan borrowing requests in October numbered 397. Last October there were only 236. In spite of our increase in borrowing, Butler has become a net lender in the national system. The effect of technology such as CD products, on-line database searching, and the OCLC system which accesses library collections nationwide, has been to greatly increase sharing of books between libraries.

## A MOVING EXPERIENCE

The Curriculum Resources Center will be relocating to the lower level of Irwin Library. Renee Reed will have her office there and will assist in the Reference Department, also. We are aware that the College of Education has become accustomed to the convenience of proximity to the Curriculum Resources Center and will do all that we can to continue to provide the same good service. The much appreciated document service will also continue. Most likely the move will be completed by January, 1990. The Media Center is no longer part of the Butler Libraries but has joined the Computer Center. It will remain in its present location.

## BURIED TREASURES

Vertical files contain more information than most people suspect. This brief exploration may serve as a guide to gems to be found in Irwin System files. In the Career Collection at Irwin Library is one file of career materials and another, still under construction, of clippings from Indianapolis Business Journal and the Star about local businesses. Across the atrium in Reference is a 'large **vertical file collection** containing information on current popular topics, Indiana and Indianapolis education, legislation, environment, economy, etc. are kept up to date with news clippings. Pamphlets, brochures, maps and booklets arrive from many sources. An index in notebook form guides the patron to the correct subject heading.

In Rare Books and Special Collections, much of Butler's past is preserved in vertical files. The largest, about 45 feet, is **biographical** material on faculty, trustees, administrators, alumni and students. Another file consists of **Faculty Assembly** minutes, memos, notes from general meetings and committee activities. **Commencement, Homecoming,** and **Graduating Classes** are each memorialized in chronological files. These three, with photographs, addresses, clippings, programs, are often used conjointly. **Fraternities, sororities,· Greek and non-Greek honorary** and **professional associations** have a file devoted to them. During the last 40 years many faculty members who received **sabbatical leaves, fellowships or grants** have contributed their finished papers, their applications, correspondence and notes to the file devoted to those records. Some applications for grants not received are also included. **Evening Division and Office of Continuing Education** has a file devoted to its work.

**The National Track and Field Hall of Fame Historical Research Library** contains four files: biography, history, photographs, sports information director brochures and pamphlets from which one could compile a team history.

In the **Science Library** ver-

tical files are often useful to alleviate freshman panic by placing relevant material into sweaty hands as a starting point before going on to indexes, card catalogs, CD indexes, etc.

Diseases, drug abuse, artificial sweeteners, Indiana related aspects of water pollution, engangered wildlife and health are popular topics. There are numerous subheadings under Pharmacy.

**Music and Fine Arts files** contain what one would expect with a few pleasant surprises in addition. The main file is indexed within that library's card catalog for efficient access. Students are the main users, but faculty sometimes find the National Endowment for the Arts grant guidelines useful. There is a separate **paintings** file arranged by artist. Individual research projects and honors theses are also kept on file. Two file-like collections kept in boxes because of their size, fragility, and value are the **Stitt Collection of Popular Music,** 1901-1964 and the **Harper Collection of Popular Music,** 1890-1970. The Stitt collection concentrates on the 20's and 30's, the Harper on the 40's.

**NEWS NOTES**

Science Citation Index is now available on CD Rom in the Science Library.

During Thanksgiving week, 5,000 additional items arrived for the Tack and Field collection.

**Irwin Reference** now has Sociofile (Sociological Abstracts 1974-1989) installed at its own workstation. There is no printer for it yet.

Our CD products are so heavily used that there are often lines of students waiting. An

appointment system may be necessary to solve the problem.

Annual Reports for selected
**foundations and organizations** are
cataloged and available for
reference use. The **telephone
book collection** has been greatly
expanded and is used frequently,
although the Indianapolis-Marion
County Public Library has the
largest phone book collection in
the state and does give information by telephone.

**Speech and English Faculty**
may want to know that the popular
Current Issues Section is expand-
ing to include Congressional
Quarterly Editorial Research
Reports, American Public Opinion
Index, Headline Series, monthly
Gallup Reports and Congressional
Digest.

**Change and Tradition Faculty**
should know that additional pertinent materials which might be
overlooked in the stacks are
being added to the subject encyclopedias and atlases in the
white cases in Reference.
General encyclopedias are at one
end on that row of cases. These
materials also provide excellent
background material for speeches
and papers.

Observers may have noticed
that continuing rearrangement of
reference materials has created
an increasingly **user-friendly
Reference** Room.

## BOOK BUDGETS

**Library liaisons** soon will
be contacting academic departments with reports on June
through November book expenditures, total amount on order, and
what amount remains to be spent.

## SUCCEEDING IN SPITE OF THE ODDS

The diagram below il-
lustrates pitfalls along the path
toward success in Reference.
Probably a similar diagram could
be designed to analyze the
teaching/learning process.

64    FALL 1989    RQ

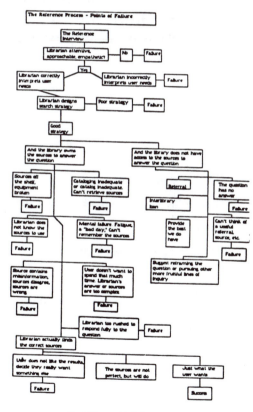

Fig. 1. Diagram of the Reference Process

LINDA HORVATH, EDITOR

# *Bookends*

## Captain John Smith Library
## Christopher Newport College

Format:  single sheet

Size:  8 1/2 by 11"

Color:  varies

Number of pages:  2

Frequency:  3 times each semester, 1 in the summer

Annual cost:  over $1,000

Number of copies:  over 1,000

Audience:  faculty, staff, administration, students, and other libraries in the state

Editorial responsibility:  rotating editor; professional librarian

Desktop software:  no

**CAPTAIN JOHN SMITH LIBRARY,** Christopher Newport College    Vol. VII, #2

## A THREE COLUMN CHEER FOR CNC LIBRARY STUDENT ASSISTANTS!

You cannot use the library without seeing them. In fact, without them, the smooth functioning of the library would be a thing of the past. What are we talking about--or who? The student assistants in the library, of course! No matter what part of the library you are using, from the card catalog to media, our student employees are here to help ensure that you have a successful trip to the library.

The first people you see when you enter the library (and the last when you leave) are the circulation assistants. These students perform a multitude of duties, including the check-in and check-out of books, servicing the copiers and the machines in microforms, collecting fines, typing overdue notices, and assisting patrons in a variety of ways. Among those you will see at the Circulation Desk are student supervisors Roberta Coviello, Cathy Nguyen, Stacey Davis, and Tarsha Thompson. They are ably assisted by John Anderson, Melissa Brodie, Renee Ford, Cheryl Vincent, Amy Williams, Shannon Bailey, Anita Burley, Jennifer Mobley, and

Clarence Washington. And without Jamie Myers and Mayra Alvarado to shelve books, we would be lost.

Whenever you need an item that a professor has placed on reserve, or if you're looking for the latest issue of your favorite magazine, or if you need an item that is only available at another college, you need the help of our periodicals assistants. Besides helping you locate the journals and reserve items you need, these students also shelve periodicals, process the new periodicals and organize reserve materials. Some also assist with interlibrary loan requests. Susan Barber, Kerry Campbell, Rita Dimmett, Samantha Ingram, Jennifer Jones, Ge Bi Len, Lisa Witten, and the four student supervisors from the Circulation Desk provide assistance whenever it is needed in the Periodicals Room.

Besides helping students locate the videos and records they need, the student assistants in Media keep busy by performing a variety of jobs. They deliver and set up media equipment in the classroom, run the laminator, and check out materials. If you need help, talk to David Penrod, Nathan Phillips, Doug Schuetz, Vera Wright, Angela Stone, Pat Silvis, Robert Kimbrel, Steve Wesen, or Sugato Chattopadhyay.

You may not see the students who work in acquisitions and cataloging, but the results of their efforts are apparent every time you use a book here. Brian Pierro and Marsha Gray are the acquisitions assistants. They have a myriad of tasks to perform, including checking in the books ordered by the faculty, filing purchase orders and invoices, notifying faculty of the arrival of approval plan books, and searching for information necessary for the ordering of books.

Without the work of the student assistants in cataloging, you might never locate the books and audiovisuals you need. Kimberly Gardner, Angela McKinney, and Dana Goldie help maintain the card catalog by filing new cards for new materials and by pulling old cards for materials no longer on the shelves. They also process trucks of materials in preparation for their placement in the stacks. When necessary, they can also do minor repairs.

As you can see, the library would not be the same without our student assistants. Thanks go to each one of them for their hard work.

## GREAT NEW FEATURE ON INFOTRAC

When you search on InfoTrac, if CNC Library has the journal cited, the message **"LIBRARY SUBSCRIBES TO JOURNAL"** appears directly below the citation on the screen and on the print-out.

## CNC LIBRARIANS' CHOICE
## A GOOD READ FOR THANKSGIVING BREAK

Browsing HQ 1397/C66/1989
Conway, Jill Ker.
**The Road From Coorain.** Knopf.

The first woman president of Smith college writes an absorbing memoir of childhood, which takes the reader from the Australian outback to the author's departure for America to attend Harvard University. A delightful tale.

Browsing PN 2287/G675/D66/1989
Donaldson, Maureen.
**An Affair to Remember.** Putnam.

An honest yet loving account of the four years Donaldson spent as Cary Grant's lover--how they met, the good times and the bad, the friendship that lasted until his death in 1986.

Browsing PR 9499.3/D465/B38/1989
Desai, Anita.
**Baumgartner's Bombay.** Knopf.

Through Baumgartner, whom we meet as a very old man, Desai makes us feel the plight of the world's outsiders. Remarkable language draws us to this representative outcast as we follow him to his inevitable doom.

Browsing PS 3558/I45/T35/1989
Hillerman, Tony.
**Talking God.** Harper and Row.

Joe Leaphorn and Jim Chee of the Navaho Tribal Police once again cross paths as a mysterious stranger is found dead near a railroad track. The mystery takes them to Washington D.C. and a museum display of native artifacts. The novel builds to a satisfying conclusion as Leaphorn and Chee save the day in our nations capital.

# *Upstairs Downstairs*

## Walter M. Pierce Library
## Eastern Oregon State College

Format:  stapled

Size:  8 1/2 by 11"

Color:  white

Number of pages:  1 - 4

Frequency:  2 - 4 per year

Annual cost:  $0 - 500

Number of copies:  150 - 300

Audience:  faculty, staff, administration, students, alumni, friends, and regional libraries

Editorial responsibility:  permanent editor; library director

Desktop software:  Mac Write

# Walter M. Pierce

## Upstairs
## Downstairs

| Volume 2 | February, 1989 | Number 3 |

**We may have three foot drifts,** an inaccessible mezzanine and the jolly pound of jackhammers, but the library is still here. Sorry for the long delay between these missals and the length of the accompanying accessions list. There's a lot of "good junk" that has been added. Come visit - we'll scrounge up a hardhat for you.

## BE A FRIEND -

Join us on Friday evening, April 14, for the charter meeting of the "Friends of the EOSC Library." It should be a fine evening, particularly with the wonderful **William Stafford** reading his poetry as our featured guest. More later on the "Friends" - time, purposes of the Friends, programs, etc. We hope you can join us.

**Our project to build** primary literary works continues - we're now adding missing items from the work of Willa Cather and William Faulkner, with about 50 more contemporary authors on our list.

**We've recently had good luck** in acquiring Oregon materials. Check the accessions list. The collecting profile has been modified by the addition of literature about Oregon and by Oregonians.

We are building on Jack Evan's fine work, and hope to have the definitive collection on our region in the near future. We solicit your help in locating donations for us.

**Speaking of good friends -** thanks to **Alliston Reid, Chuck Coate, Dee Caputo, Jim Hottois** and, particularly, **Mary Jane Loso** for their gifts - Dr. Loso gave us 617 volumes of exceptionally worthwhile primary and secondary literary materials; nearly all of which we did not previously have.

**By the time you get this,** the mezzanine book area should be open again - thanks for your cooperation during the closure. Access to the area is now only through KEOL space and the construction area, across the new cement floor where the old stairs were. **Please use care.** It looks like the completion date for the NEW ENTRANCE will be pushed forward to April or so, due to the unexpected amount of white fluff and cold.

**A new reference set** of interest, received from the International Trade Institute at PSU - Trade Flow Tables, gives import and export figures for Oregon, Washington, and the Northwest on 46 commodity groups from 1983 through June '88. (Ref HF3161.07 T8 1988)

# PEOPLE & PLACES

**Doug O.** attended an OCLC Directors' Conference in Portland on the new OCLC system; **Theresa S.** has been appointed to a Task Force of EOLS, to coordinate the implementation of the 5-year plan to convert all book records in the region to MR form; **Patty C.** attended the Oregon CRLA and was a presenter at Oregon On-Line last week; **Mary F.** attended a searching workshop and has been heavily involved in the OLA work to submit needs to the legislature; **Doug** braved the storms to attend an OSSHE Interlibrary Council meeting in Eugene; **Patty** consulted on SRS in Montana and participated in an Admissions trip; **Suz E.** journeyed to Portland to receive a computer program for audiovisual control; and **Susan G.** and **Patty** investigated an automated overdue system at BMCC.

# BITS & PIECES

**We now have an index** to all of the H. L. Davis material at the U. of Texas (thanks, Jim Brown) - Earl Van Brokland of La Grande gave us several copies of turn-of-the-century plot maps, deeds, and farming reminiscences - the EMC has added quite a few new videos to the collection, inclusing: You Make the Difference: Preventing Home Burglary, and

Oregon: State of Wonder - the Library has added eight reference volumes on Jewish history and culture, courtesy of the Jewish Chautauqua Society - congratulations to our intern, Sylvia Bonebrake Bowers, who tied the knot with Bruce on 12/27 (she also is now involved in cataloging the Micronesian materials in that office) - effective at the end of Winter Term, the fine system will uniformly apply to all students, faculty, and staff.

**Another step toward an integrated computer system** in the Library - **Suz End** has obtained a program from SOSC for control of audiovisual procedures, has modified it, and now has the first aspect (classroom equipment scheduling) in operation. Several other procedures will soon follow. Three library integrated system components now are operational, and we're investigating equipment for the rest, and strategies for funding them.

**Please Note:** the EMC now requires a minimum of one hour's notice for requests pertaining to AV equipment delivery, set-up and/or pick-up - call Suz, ext. **1388,** as far in advance as possible to arrange for your AV equipment needs.

**Grants, grants, grants!** We have submitted several that could bring us much needed growth help. **Patty** has written an application for a federal title II D award that would bring us CD-ROM technology for extending the SRS service and for local use. **Doug** has gotten by the first hurdle on a LSCA grant for an automated serials control system that would access every periodical in Eastern Oregon. **Patty** has written another, on behalf of the E. O. Library Association, to bring computers to those libraries in the region without them. **Mary F.** is working on another EOLA grant for converting library records to MR form. **We still await the arrival** of our Macintosh

30

CD-ROM system from OCLC, with high expectations. We are a test site for OCLC as they develop this system. February / March looks about right.

**Seen or heard of a good book** you would like to read? We can get anything for you. Now that we have a full-timer in the Interlibrary Loan position, we can better serve you. **Joanne Nelson** is a great addition, and welcomes your requests **(x1735)**, or see the Circulation Desk.

**We still await the publication of** <u>Books for College Libraries III</u> - with trembling hands, as it will provide us with a quality, up-to-date bibliography of a 55,000 volume collection for a liberal arts college. We hope to print out buying lists of non-held materials for every discipline.

**Faculty and staff** - remember that the library electronic mail system connects the three college campuses in the region, and that messages can be delivered through those libraries and the network.

# Happy Schussing!

# *Nash News*

## Nash Library
## Gannon University

Format: folder

Size: 8 1/2 by 11"

Color: buff

Number of pages: 1 - 4

Frequency: irregular

Annual cost: $500 - 1,000

Number of copies: 300 - 500

Audience: faculty, staff, administration, students, and friends

Editorial responsibility: permanent editor;secretary

Desktop software: VAX word processing

# NASH NEWS

## The Nash Library

**Vol. 1, No. 3**  **GANNON UNIVERSITY**  **April 3, 1989**

## National Library Week is April 9-15

This year's National Library Week celebration focuses on the importance of the librarian to our "information society." Using the theme, "Ask a Professional. Ask Your Librarian," the campaign aims to educate the public about the role of librarians and promote the visibility of the profession.

In recent years, librarians have expressed growing concern about their image, and their need to attract young people to library careers. The problem in trying to "clean up" the image is that the more librarians protest the stereotype, the more it is applied. To combat this problem, the American Library Association has launched their National Library Week campaign with an emphasis on a real consumer benefit, getting information. Reminding the public that librarians are masters at helping people get information quickly emphasizes their extremely valuable service, a service that will be even more important in the future.

In the Nash Library we believe the librarian should be "the accessible human resource" of the information age. In an academic library especially, service to our students is our foremost professional goal. The theme says it eloquently, yet simply: "Ask a professional. Ask your Librarian."

## Nash Library Honors Graduating Work-Study Students

Nash Library is fortunate to have a large and capable group of work-study students. Without work-study help the Library could not remain open for the hours it does, nor could it attempt major projects like reclassifying the collection or qualitative evaluation of the collection. Many work-studies come to us in their freshman year and remain with us until they graduate.

We'd like to say "thank you" to our work-study students who will graduate in May:

**Terry Malloy** - Terry has worked in both Microforms and Reference since the summer of 1987. A finance major from Butler, Pennsylvania, she is looking forward to work in the field of banking.

**Karen Bost** - Karen has worked in Circulation since the spring of 1987. A marketing major from North Huntingdon, she expects to spend the summer planning her October 1989 wedding. She and her future husband will live in Virginia.

**Chris Burckhart** - Chris works in Microforms this semester, but she previously worked in Periodicals for two and one-half years. A chemistry-biology major from Aliquippa, Chris is looking forward to working in a laboratory in the Pittsburgh area.

**John Pennsy** - John has been a mainstay of the Circulation Department for all four of his years at Gannon. An accounting major from Erie, John is looking forward to work involving accounting or finance. He hopes to stay in the Erie area.

Working with these students has been a pleasure. We wish them successful futures filled with happiness, and we hope they will remember fondly their years at the Nash Library.

## Vax Terminals in Reference Pave the Way to Computerization

Two VAX computer terminals were placed near the card catalog in the Reference Department last fall as a way of taking the Library's first step toward eventual computerization. One of the terminals holds a list of all items that have been placed on reserve by faculty members. Faculty reserves can be brought up by professor's last name, course number, or call number of the item. The other terminal can list all of the periodicals titles owned by the Nash Library, as well as list of Computer Center resources and the Old Farmers Almanac.

The faculty reserve list is the result of a program created by a student worker last summer. The other terminal, with its main menu, is part of Videotext, a facility available on the University's mainframe computer.

Future planning calls for the Nash Library's collections to be placed on a database that can be searched using VAX terminals throughout the University. With campus-wide access to the Library's collections, students and faculty alike would benefit from the convenience of computerization. When a library user is able to search a database for specific subject areas, he or she has a more comprehensive and accurate use of library materials than a card catalog search would permit. Computerized search of the collections would certainly broaden students' research capability, since it would provide an exhaustive and precise means of exploring any topic.

### New Titles

Boas, Nancy, The society of six: California colorists. ND/1351.6/.B63/1988

Sansone, David, Greek athletics and the genesis of sport. GV/706.8/.S26/1988

Gardner, Lloyd, Approaching Vietnam: from World War II through Dienbienphu, 1941-1956. E/183.8/.V5/G36/1988

Brinkle, Lydle, An American's guide to the Soviet Union. DK/16/.B75/1988

Bosticco, Mary, Personal letters for business people. PE/1483/.B67/1986

Davies, Hugh Sykes, Wordsworth and the worth of words. PR/5894/.D38/1986

Hollywood and history: costume design in film. PN/1955.9/.C56/H65/1987

Rybakov, Anatoli N., Children of the Arbat. PG/3476/.R87/D4813/1988

## What Number Should I Call...?

We often get calls from people who don't know which department of the Library will handle their specific request. Some often-asked questions (and their answers) are:

-How do I reserve a room on the Library's lower level? Call Ginny Caldwell in the Media Center, x7560.

-Can the general public borrow books from the Library? What is the procedure? Call the Circulation Department, x7557.

-To whom do I talk to about setting up library tours and putting books on reserve? Call Bob Dobiesz, x7558.

-How do I find a publisher's address? Call Susan Smith, x7763.

-How do I use the FAX machine? Call the Reference Department, x7559.

If you have a different "what number should I call..." question that might be of general interest, please send it to the Library, Nash News, and we'll answer it in the next issue.

Curran, Charles E., Tensions in moral theology. BJ/1249/.C83/1988

Knystautas, Algirdas, The natural history of the USSR. QH/161/.K55/1987

Winfree, Arthur T., The timing of biological clocks. QH/527/.W56/1987

Stechert, Kathryn, Sweet success: how to understand the men in your business life - and win with your own rules. HD/6053/.S724/1986

Nathan, Richard, Reagan and the states. HJ/2051/.N167/1987

Laquer, Walter, The age of terrorism. HV/6431/.L36/1987

Clearing the air: perspectives on environmental tobacco smoke. TD/883.1/.C58/1988

Gribbin, John R., The hole in the sky: man's threat to the ozone layer. TD/885.5/.O85/G75/1988

## Cataloging Department Prepares Books for Shelves

The cartoon beside this article shows a librarian working to assign call numbers to books. Loosely taken, it may seem funny, but here at the Nash Library this cartoon is anything but accurate. Cataloging is precise work that calls for technical expertise and strict attention to detail.

Now that we have adopted the Library of Congress system of cataloging, the cataloger and the cataloging technicians make full use of OCLC, the Online Computer Library Center, which provides a database of cataloging information. A new or gift book will go through the following steps in cataloging:

- Technicians search the OCLC database and make a printed record of the cataloging information that matches that book.

- Each printout is checked for accuracy. Since the record does not always match the book, sometimes the printout must be edited. At this point series information is checked, subject headings updated, and any additional information added. At this point the book is considered cataloged.

- Technicians produce catalog cards and the computer record is added to our database of OCLC holdings. Now whenever that book is searched on OCLC, the record will show us that we own the book. Also, whenever anyone on the national OCLC system asks for a "display holdings" on that book, it will show that Gannon University owns it. This information is quite useful for interlibrary loan purposes.

At this point, processing begins:

- Technicians type cards and pockets for the books as well as writing in the call number and the source line.

- Work-study assistants install security strips, type spine labels, and apply labels to the books that have been cataloged. Once this last step has been checked, the book moves on to circulation to be shelved and available for student use.

Father Snyderwine. Director of the Library, serves as Head of Technical Services. Pamela Reed, Head Cataloger and Associate Head of Technical Services, does all original (non-OCLC) cataloging. She works closely with the cataloging technicians to answer (continued)

*"And this is the fellow who assigns LC catalog card numbers to new books."*

(Cataloging continued)
questions, assist with OCLC problems, and provide professional guidance and consistency to the Library's cataloging. The daily goal of the three cataloging technicians is to catalog 60 "reclass" books (changing from Dewey call numbers to Library of Congress) and 15 new and gift books. With more than 200,000 volumes to reclassify, the Cataloging Department can't look forward to a "slow season!"

(Next month: Like the New York Times, Our *Circulation* is Great!)

## New Periodical Titles Added

Lawrence Maxted, Periodicals Librarian, indicates that the following new titles have been added to our collection:

American Demographics
Canadian Journal of Radiation Technology
Contemporary Physics
Direct Marketing
Industrial Marketing Management
Journal of Accounting and Economics
Journal of Basic Writing
Journal of Family Psychology
Journal of Recreational Mathematics
Mac World
Man and World
Mathematical Intelligencer
Publish
Respiratory Care
Security Mangement
Written Communication

## Pundles

A pundle is a puzzle combined with a riddle.  For  example:

MUCH    SOON        =      TOO MUCH TOO SOON
MUCH    SOON

Can you figure out these ones? If not, you'll find the answers in the
Reference Department of the Nash Library.

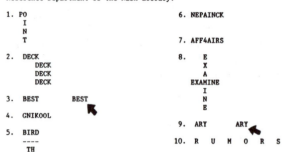

1. PO
   I
   N
   T

2. DECK
      DECK
      DECK
      DECK

3. BEST    BEST

4. GNIKOOL

5. BIRD
   ----
   TH

6. NEPAINCK

7. AFF4AIRS

8. E
   X
   A
   EXAMINE
   I
   N
   E

9. ARY    ARY

10. R  U  M  O  R  S

---

## Microforms Librarian Heads PLA Intellectual Freedom Committee

Gerard Laurito, Microforms Librarian, is currently
serving as State Chair of the Pennsylvania Library
Association's Intellectual Freedom Committee. The
committee consists of an appointed chairperson and
a repesentative from each chapter of the PLA, and
its purpose is to advocate freedom of selection of
materials for libraries of all types and sizes. The
committee exists to offer a network of support to
local libraries whose acquisitions policies are chal-
lenged, and it offers the legitimacy of state and national affiliation (through ALA) to any library who
faces a censorship battle.

The committee recently revised the PLA's
*Intellectual Freedom Handbook,* which provides collection development guidelines that encourage freedom and challenge censorship for all libraries. The
*Handbook* includes a "Freedom to Read" statement
as well as policies on labeling, restricted access, con-
fidentiality, and an especially pertinent section on
"Sexism, Racism, and Other -Isms in Library
Materials."

The committee has tackled another controversial
issue: the choice of feature films to be loaned by libraries. Should libraries purchase "uncut" feature
films for circulation, or should the expurgated ver-
sions that may be less artistically satisfying be purchased?

(Microforms Librarian continued)

The freedom to read is essential to our democracy,
and the Intellectual Freedom Committee provides a
forum for discussion of topics that are basic to that
freedom. Questions relevant to the work of the committee may be directed to Gerry Laurito, 871-7553,
at the Nash Library.

*The Nash News*
Vol. 1, No. 3 April 3, 1989
Editor: Loretta Brandon

Nash News is a publication of Gannon
University's Nash Library, 619 Sassafras
Street, Erie, PA 16541.
Telephone: (814) 871-7552.
Type has been set using VAX DECpage facility.
Nash Library hours are:

   Monday-Thursday, 8 A.M. to midnight
   Friday, 8 A.M. to 4:30 P.M.
   Saturday, 10-4:30
   Sunday, 1-midnight

Hours vary during semester breaks.
For additional information, please call (814) 871-
7552.

# *Mnemosyne*

## Julia Rogers Library
## Goucher College

Format: folder

Size: 8 1/2 by 11"

Color: buff

Number of pages: 4

Frequency: 2 - 4 per semester

Annual cost: $0 - 500

Number of copies: over 1,000

Audience: faculty, staff, administration, and students

Editorial responsibility: rotating editor; currently library director and secretary

Desktop software: Word Perfect 5.0

# Mnemosyne

*A Newsletter of the Julia Rogers Library*
*Goucher College                Towson, Maryland*

*Volume 3          Number 2          October 1989*

## FROM THE LIBRARIAN

One of the best bargains on campus is the library noontime series.  For the investment of 30 minutes you can hear members of the Goucher community talk about current research, read their poetry or perform music. Occasionally we also show a film. The setting is informal and all are welcome. Schedules are available in the library.  If you would like to volunteer or suggest a speaker, please drop me a note or stop by my office.

Thanks are due to the anonymous student whose phone call alerted us to the presence in Pearlstone of a box of books and periodicals which had been missing from the library since 1987 (before the security system!)  We're happy to have them back.

If you haven't read Darcey Steinke's book, reviewed elsewhere in this issue, check for it on the new book shelf. I've just finished it and heartily recommend it.

Our November exhibit will illustrate world events of the year 1789.

—NM

## WHAT'S NEW IN THE LIBRARY

### TRIAL RUN FOR BUSINESS AND NEWSPAPER ABSTRACT CD-ROMS

The library is trying out two new CDROM products: ABI/INFORM Ondisc and Newspaper Abstracts Ondisc. The trial period started on October 11 and will last for 60 days. The workstation for these products is next to the AV room door.  The library staff would like you to try out the products and let us know whether we should keep them.    Just fill out an evaluation form near the workstation and drop it off at the reference desk.

The Newspaper Abstracts database is similar to the INFOTRAC National Newspaper CD-ROM. They both index the New York Times, Wall Street Journal, Washington Post, Christian Science Monitor, and Los Angeles Times; and both products allow you to print out the citations. The Newspaper Abstracts does more. It indexes additional newspapers--the Chicago Tribune, the Boston Globe, and the Atlanta Constitution; and it provides short summaries of the newspaper stories.    It has more sophisticated search options which may be confusing at first, but which can be figured out by using Help screens or asking a reference librarian for help.

ABI/NFORM is a similar product which indexes over 800 business and management journals using the same searching techniques.

−YL

## *THE BOOK REVIEW*

816      UP THROUGH THE WATER,
S822Ju    by Darcey Steinke
           (Doubleday, 1989)

Darcey Steinke, a 1985 graduate of Goucher College, has produced a first novel that has been well-received in critical circles. UP THROUGH THE WATER is a short book, and one which is notable for its fluid , poetic language. The story is about Emily, who lives on Ocracoke, and Eddie, her 16-year-old son, who lives during the year with his father and stepmother, but comes to spend the summers with her. Emily is deeply tied to the water, from whence the title of the book derives, and her connection to water is far more real to her than her daily existence. She is also "in love," as much as her nature will allow, with two men: John Berry, a ferryman who drinks too much and is prone to violence, and Birdflower, a short order cook with a long braid who fancies himself a relic of the 60s. Eddie experiences his first love during this summer also, with Lila, an island girl who rides wild horses and is determined to marry off the island of her birth.

The story, which covers their experiences and feelings over the summer, could be read to be slight. We read not so much of plot and character development as we do of imageries and colors. The story coheres much as an impressionist painting, with a language which -- if viewed at a distance -- does tell something. The reader is struck at first more by the prose itself than the story it tells. Near the opening of the

work, we read of Emily swimming in the ocean: "Each stroke let a million thin swords of pale green light into the water. Emily began rotating, looking out to the horizon, a double feature in blue, sky and water, then face into the sea, bubbles delicately nudging her cheek. Each stroke was something: a faceless baritone voice in the dark, the oleander berries that grew around the cottage, the smell of power, a baby-blue scarf she used to wear in her hair...." Even the gory death of a pony, which Lila must drown to put out of misery, comes out poetically: "Eddie let the horse go. It sank down a little, the tide moved it. Blood from the cut leg swirled thick and greasy around him." Steinke's novel, though brief, takes time to read if one is to fully absorb the beauty of its content.

(After graduation from Goucher, Steinke received a masters degree from the University of Virginia, has worked at the White House, and spent a year in Ireland. She is at work on a second novel.)

−TL

## *NEW AND INTERESTING BOOKS*

| | |
|---|---|
| 791.43<br>B415 | BEFORE HOLLYWOOD:<br>Turn-of-the-century<br>American film |
| 910.92<br>B619s | Birkett, Dea<br>SPINSTERS ABROAD:<br>Victorian Lady Explorers |
| 574.19<br>C928S | Crick, Francis<br>WHAT MAD PURSUIT:<br>a Personal View of<br>Scientific Discovery |
| 816<br>C952Jt | Cross, Amanda<br>A TRAP FOR FOOLS |
| 738.973<br>E93a | Everson Museum of Art<br>AMERICAN CERAMICS |

839.16      Hagerfors, Lennart
H144JvBh    THE WHALES IN LAKE
            TANGANYIKA

Ref.        THE INSIDER'S GUIDE TO
378.73      THE COLLEGES - 1989
1591

782.42A     PRAIRIE HOME COMPANION
P898        FOLK SONG BOOK

816         Reed, Ishmael
R3241Kw     WRITIN' IS FIGHTIN':
            Thirty-seven years
            of Boxing on Paper

## THEY HAVE SHEET MUSIC IN THE RARE BOOK ROOM?

Next time you are trying to track down popular tunes from the early twentieth century, think of the college's Rare Book Room. Thanks to the Rev. Virgil Van Street, an Episcopal clergymen who died in September at the age of 82, the college has a wonderful collection of popular sheet music published from 1898 to the middle 1950s.

The collection was built by Mr. Van Street's first wife, Irma Simpler, and many of the 500-odd pieces bear her signature. The music, most of which is scored for voice and piano, ranges from patriotic war songs to show tunes. In a day before most people owned phonographs, the market for sheet music of popular songs was enormous, and the scores were sold much as records are now; with colorful colors, lots of advertising, and the lyricists and composers (not the performers) featured prominently.

The collector, Irma Simpler Van Street, died in 1968. At the time, Mr. Van Street, who had been a prosecutor in the Nuremberg War Crimes Trials, was a 61-year-old lawyer with 20 years in the

foreign service. He retired, went back to school, and in 1971 was ordained an Episcopal clergyman. While serving several churches in Maryland in the 1970s, he gave the Simple/Van Street collection of sheet music to the Goucher College Library. Ultimately Rev. Van Street retired to Florida in 1980.

The library has drawn up a card file of the sheet music collection, and the music is stored in acid-free folders in the rare book room. Stop by and see it next time you have a hankering for Come On Papa (1918), The Honolulu Blues (1923), Scatter-Brain(1939), The Shepherd Serenade (1941), or any of several hundred other pop tunes of days gone by.
–SH

## MORE MUSIC TREASURES

Tucked away in the library's audio-visual area is a small collection of phonograph records which pre-date the era of long-playing and compact discs. Known as 78's, indicating the rate at which they revolved on the turntable, these records were for decades state of the art. Then came LP's and now CD's. Heavy and fragile when compared with the long playing records which superseded them, the 78's were gradually withdrawn from the library's extensive collection.

Such world famous artists as Casals, Galli-Curci, Chaliapin and Ponselle are represented and there are composers such as Prokofieff, Gershwin and Rachmaninoff playing their own works. Although most of the records are musical there are spoken word gems by H. L. Mencken, Maurice Evans and George Bernard Shaw among others.

No longer in the mainstream because of their ·fragility, these records may be listened to if special arrangements aremade through the audio-visualoffice.
–MB

## LOOK UP THE FACTS!!! DON'T GET LEFT BEHIND!

### *NEW REFERENCE BOOKS*

The following books are recent additions to our reference collection. Some are new editions and some are new titles for the library.

Merck Manual, 15th edition.
Ref 615.5 M555 The latest edition of the standard guide to all your medical problems. (Have your medical dictionary handy!!)

American Statistics Index.
Ref 317.3 A512 Index Authoritative answers to your "how many" or "how much" questions, a location tool and guide to all those statistics in government documents.

The Guinness Book of World Records.
Ref 032 G964 1989 The book to use if you should want to know the highest speed recorded on a skateboard, or the name of the wrestler who received the most money for a single bout.

Encyclopedia of Southern Culture.
Ref 974.1 E56 Arranged in broad subject areas (agriculture, literature, recreation, violence, etc.) with topics alphabetical within each area; a good general index.

Historical Dictionary of North American Archeology. Ref 970.01 H673
A source to use to find out that Calvert Point is not a place, and that the Los Angeles Skeleton is not one left over from prohibition days! —BAS

### *RETROSPECTIVE CONVERSION*

Will Goucher ever have an online catalog? Yes – we're working very hard to prepare for it.

Cataloging of library materials since December 1982 has been done on OCLC (a bibliographic utility). Not only have we received cards for our card catalog but a machine readable cataloging (MARC) record has been stored on tapes. However, before we have a complete data base we must convert the catalog record for all of those books we acquired between 1885 and 1982.

We began this Retrospective Conversion process in early 1985 using OCLC online in more economical non-prime time. In March 1989, to further reduce costs we were able to obtain MIcrocon software from OCLC to enter data onto discs that will be matched against their database. Items that retrieve more than one record will be reviewed either from data sheets sent to us or online and then re-entered. Items with no match will be cataloged and entered into the OCLC database by Goucher's Catalog Librarian. There is much reviewing that needs to be done at various times to create a clean database.

To date we have cataloged online 24,408 titles, converted online 46,473 titles, and entered data for 13,142 titles onto disks. Because our collection numbers about 250,000, there is much work yet to be done. With a greatly increased number of new titles to be cataloged and processed, we are also limited in the time we can devote to this process. But we continue to move toward the goal of automation, confident that, like the tortoise, we will finish the race!
    —ELJ

# *Bookbytes**

## Van Wylen Library
## Hope College

Format: folder

Size: 5 3/4 by 8 1/2"

Color: varies

Number of pages: 4

Frequency: irregular, approximately 4 per semester

Annual cost: n.a.

Number of copies: 300 - 500

Audience: faculty, staff, administration, students, and retired professionals living in the area

Editorial responsibility: editorial board; professional librarians and staff

Desktop software: no

*The nameplate is printed commercially on heavy stock. The text is photocopied in a campus printing facility.

# Bookbytes

a newsletter published by the
Hope College Libraries

Volume 5, Number 3, February 1990

## THANK YOU FOR NOT SMOKING

Van Wylen Library is now a completely smoke-free building. A no smoking policy will be enforced in all areas of the building, including the lounge area on the first floor. This action was taken following numerous complaints from library patrons who were unable to use the lounge due to the unhealthy smoke-filled conditions. It was also discouraging to enter a brand new facility and be confronted with the distinct odor of stale smoke. In addition, the careless behavior of some smokers has caused permanent damage to the woodwork, furniture, and carpet in the lounge. The staff realizes that this policy will inconvenience a few of our patrons; however, our overriding concern is to promote a healthy environment for all library users and to preserve the quality of the library building.

## LIBRARY AUTOMATION IMPROVEMENTS

The Acquisitions component of the integrated library system is now functioning. Materials being considered for order, as well as materials already on order, appear in the Public Access Catalog. This exciting addition will allow departments to make more informed book selection decisions, and will let everyone anticipate material that is on its way to the library. Records for materials on order appear in capital letters and the status indicates that the item is "on order."

Other system improvements include a software upgrade which improved the library system response time and replaced the six character codes in Boolean searching with locations spelled out in plain English. Computer Services has also changed the way in which the public terminals are logged in, making all the terminals more readily available. To reconnect a disconnected terminal, users should press the return key until the menu appears. It is no longer necessary to ask for assistance in order to bring the terminal back online.

## UNUSUAL BIBLE DONATED TO THE LIBRARY

Everett Welmers, whose personal donations have done so much to develop the special and rare book collections at Hope, has given us another rare book. Dr. Welmers (class of 1932) has presented the Van Wylen Library with a two volume Greek New Testament published in Amsterdam in 1751–52. This is an unusual edition because it includes extensive critical commentary as footnotes (in Latin) by Johann Jakob Wetstein (or Wettstein) interspersed with the Greek New Testament text that was originally printed by Elzevier. The Wetstein Greek New Testament will be shelved in the Rare Book Room on the ground floor of the Van Wylen Library.

## VIDEO RECORDINGS IN THE LIBRARY

Videocassettes are one of the fastest growing collections in the library; they now number over 300. The availability of excellent playback facilities for groups and individuals has prompted faculty to order more videos for use by their classes. Some departments have transferred their video collections to the library, making them more accessible to students and faculty.

To search for a specific video title in the Public Access Catalog, you should qualify your search by material type. To do this type T=[title], a vertical line, followed by an M=gm and RETURN. For example: T=Hamlet |m=gm.

To browse through Van Wylen's entire video collection, enter the Keyword/Boolean searching mode. At the > prompt type F1 videocassette or videorecording.

For faculty who do not have access to the online catalog in their offices, a printed catalog of the library's video collection has been distributed to each department.

Faculty may make arrangements to show videos to groups in the Granberg Room by calling our library secretary at 7790. Three carrels with playback equipment and monitors are also available for use by individuals. Videos circulate to faculty for seven days, but are only available to students for use in Van Wylen.

## USE OF VAN WYLEN LIBRARY CONTINUES TO INCREASE

During our first year in Van Wylen use of the library increased dramatically. This was not a surprise, although the rate of increase exceeded our expectations. We were surprised, however, that use continued to increase in 1989 at a pace faster than it had increased in 1988.

During July through December 1989 the library experienced a 32.4% increase in out-of-building circulation, a 104% increase of interlibrary borrowing, and a 100% increase in reference inquiries over the previous fall. Out-of-building circulation for the calendar year 1989 increased 62.5% over the last calendar year (1987) that we spent in Van Zoeren. The new building, the automated catalog and circulation systems, and the Lilly Grant program have all contributed to advanced use of library resources. We are delighted that these improvements and programs have resulted in better use of the material and human library resources at Hope. We will continue our efforts to bring you the very best library service possible.

## CHANGES IN NEW BOOKS INFORMATION

The shift to an automated acquisition system has eliminated the use of the multiple part forms that were used in ordering books. The lack of these forms means that persons who order books will no longer receive copies indicating that the book was ordered (white) or that it had been cataloged (goldenrod). We will continue to send goldenrod colored slips until the books in the manual order file have all been received. We also produce a monthly acquisition list to help keep you informed of books newly cataloged.

Those of you who regularly peruse the new books shelves will want to know that we don't always have room to display every new book after it has been processed. Occasionally we catalog so many books in a week that we can't fit them on the available shelves. At those times we will need to send some of the new books directly to the stacks. We will also reduce the length of time new books are exhibited to allow as many volumes as possible to be displayed.

## VAN WYLEN LIBRARY RECEIVES ANOTHER AWARD

Pioneer Construction and Hope College were honored in November by the Associated Builders and Contractors, West Michigan Chapter with an Award of Excellence for the construction of the Van Wylen Library.

VAN WYLEN LIBRARY, HOPE COLLEGE

## NEW COMPACT DISCS IN THE LIBRARY

The library has acquired two new bibliographic databases on compact discs which will allow students and faculty to perform their own database searches at no charge. Using the SilverPlatter Information System to search the PsycLit and ERIC databases allows one to use keyword and boolean search techniques to review the literature in each database from 1974 to the present.

The PsycLit database is synonymous to the print Psychological Abstracts and contains citations and summaries of the world's periodical literature in psychology and related subjects. PsycLit is contained on two compact discs, one covering 1983 to the present and the other containing 1974–1982.

The ERIC database contains two files, Resources in Education (RIE) and the Current Index to Journals in Education (CIJE). Resources in Education provides citations and abstracts to the document literature of education including research reports, curriculum guides, conference papers, etc. Current Index to Journals in Education provides citations and abstracts to articles from 740 major educational and education related journals.

Faculty who are interested in having their students use either PsycLit or ERIC on compact disc, may schedule a group or in-class training session with one of the reference librarians. The sessions are designed to review the basics of constructing a search as well as the mechanics and commands used to search the SilverPlatter system.

To receive individual training or more information about PsycLit or ERIC on compact disc, contact Kelly Jacobsma at 7791.

## STAFF CHANGES

Patti Carlson has joined the Van Wylen Library staff as secretary. She will continue the time-share arrangement with Mimi Beukema and work Monday, Wednesday, and Friday. Patti replaces Marge Clark who, after nearly ten years at the library, decided to devote more time to her real estate business.

Patti Carlson comes to us with experience as a medical and as a church secretary. We're delighted to have her with us. Please come in and get acquainted with both Mimi and Patti.

48

# *Loyola University Library Newsletter*

## Loyola University Library
## Loyola University

Format: folder

Size: 8 1/2 by 11"

Color: buff

Number of pages: 4 - 6

Frequency: quarterly

Annual cost: not known

Number of copies: over 1,000

Audience: faculty, staff, administration, students, alumni, and friends

Editorial responsibility: permanent editor; professional librarian

Desktop software: Pagemaker

# Loyola University Library
# *Newsletter*

New Series, no.6          Fall 1989

## Did You Check Out a Book in 88/89?
### A look at circulation figures in the Main Library by patron type

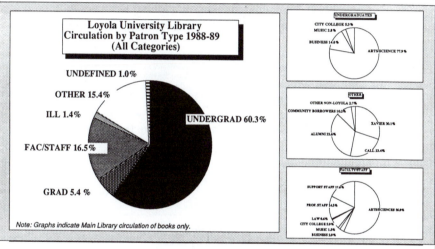

Loyola University Library
Circulation by Patron Type 1988-89
(All Categories)

UNDEFINED 1.0%
OTHER 15.4%
ILL 1.4%
UNDERGRAD 60.3%
FAC/STAFF 16.5%
GRAD 5.4%

Note: Graphs indicate Main Library circulation of books only.

UNDERGRADUATES
CITY COLLEGE 5.3%
MUSIC 2.1%
BUSINESS 14.6%
ARTS/SCIENCE 77.9%

OTHER
OTHER NON-LOYOLA 2.7%
COMMUNITY BORROWERS 10.2%
ALUMNI 33.6%
XAVIER 30.1%
CALL 23.4%

FACULTY/STAFF
SUPPORT STAFF 17.6%
PROF. STAFF 14.5%
ARTS/SCIENCES 56.9%
LAW 0.6%
CITY COLLEGE 5.5%
MUSIC 1.3%
BUSINESS 2.9%

## Library Use Tops Half Million

For the first time, use of the Main, Miller, and Music Libraries has topped half a million . Patrons are counted automatically as they leave the libraries, and in 1988-89 the combined count reached 517,000, as compared to 452,258 in 1987-88. The surge in use is attributed to increased use of library and media center services and collections and the great popularity of the Miller and Music microlabs.

Circulation of books and other materials continued to climb, reaching an all time high of 86,331, up from 82,513 in 1987-88. In 1988-89 well over 28,000 questions were answered by library staff. Loyola Library shared its resources, sending a record 1,345 books and periodical articles to other libraries through the interlibrary loan service (ILL).

In 1988-89, materials available through the Library's online catalog grew as bibliographic records for new materials were added to the database and over 10,000 records for older materials were converted to machine readable form. The project to add serial titles to *LUCI* resulted in the addition of music periodicals to the database.

The acquisitions approval plan was refined and in the fall of 1988 led to the quick delivery of many newly published materials needed by faculty and students.

In the spring and summer of 1989 the Library's solicitation of gifts and donations to the collection bolstered its resources.

*-Mary Lee Sweat*
*University Librarian*

### Inside:

*Adopt -A -Book Program*
*Books In Brief*
*Business Research*
*News*
*Who's Reading What*
*and more...*

# In The Music Library...

The 1989-90 New Orleans Symphony and Opera discographies should be available soon. They'll be posted in the hanging blue files near the circulation desk, and everyone is welcome to pick up a copy. These free guides list the repertoire planned for both organizations this season, along with recordings, scores and books on these pieces owned by the Loyola Music Library.

*Remember:* compact discs, scores and non-reference books on these lists may be checked out by patrons with a Loyola library bar code. And, of course, all patrons are welcome to use the materials in the Music Library as well (we have complete audiovisual facilites including a VCR and compact disc players).

We'd like to say a special word of thanks to all those who chose the Music Library for their monetary gift through the recent *"Adopt-A-Book"* campaign. Due to the generosity of donors, we have been able to purchase two videos (one with New Orleans' own Wynton Marsalis, the other an opera) plus three music scores.

-*Laura Dankner*
*Music Librarian*

---

Loyola University Library
*Newsletter*

Published by Loyola University Library
Mary Lee Sweat, University Librarian
Deborah Poole, Editor & Layout Design
Send all inquiries to:
Loyola University Library
6363 St. Charles Avenue, Box 198
New Orleans, LA 70118

---

## New News News News News News News News News

## New CDs Improve Library Services for Researchers

The Library has recently acquired two new systems on compact disc which should be of great help to University and community researchers. The **InfoTrac** system has been enhanced by the addition of the **Government Publications Index.** The same workstations which give easy access to periodicals can now provide the same type of access to government documents.

This summer saw the debut of **ERIC on disc,** a CD index to ERIC documents and journal articles in education. While this tool is geared most directly to those looking for information on education, it is highly useful in a variety of other areas of study, including psychology and communications. This system gives the researcher almost as much power as an online search, and with quarterly updates, the information base is kept quite current.

## New Librarian Joins Reference Department

On September 11, **Jim Hobbs,** seven year veteran and Science Reference Librarian of the University of New Orleans will join the Reference Department as the new Reference Librarian/Online Services Coodinator. Jim will be filling the vacancy left by **Eric Scholl.** Eric, who was with the department for two and half years and who contributed so much in teaching library users about the new online catalog, has become a research librarian for Bentix Aerospace in the San Francisco Bay Area. **We wish Eric much success and welcome Jim to Loyola.**

## Head of Reference Speaks to *Score* Seminar

On July 11, Mark Sutton, Head of Reference at Loyola's Main Library, spoke at a seminar held by SCORE (Service Corps of Retired Executives) for those interested in starting their own businesses. Mark spoke on resources and services available at the Loyola University Library which would be of interest to community entrepreneurs. SCORE holds these seminars each month, and Mark hopes to become a regular speaker at the meetings.

## University Library Visiting Committee Members Receive Top Awards

At the American Library Association annual conference held in June in Dallas, Library Visiting Committee members received special recognition. **Alex Allain was honored as a founder and long time supporter of the Freedom to Read Foundation, and Paulette Holahan received the ALA Citation of Merit to Trustees.** This Citation is awarded annually to the "outstanding library trustee in the United States." Congratulations!

Congratulations are also in order for Visiting Committee member **Walker Percy, who received an honorary degree and the prestigious Laetare Medal from the University of Notre Dame.**

## The air that we breathe, the water that we drink...

An exhibit concerning environmental issues will be on display in the Miller Hall Library October 1. The exhibit will feature books, government documents, newspaper articles and pictures illustrating such issues as ozone depletion, water pollution, and acid rain. A bibliography will be available for those interested in reading on these important issues. Ideas for library exhibits are always welcome; write to *Loyola Library Newsletter,* Box 198.

# Adopt-A-Book Program

**Thank you** to the many friends who have taken part in Loyola University Library's *Adopt-A-Book Program*. The program is a **project of the Loyola University Library Visiting Committee,** Verna Landrieu, chair, and is led by a committee composed of Nash Roberts, chair, Tony Gagliano, and Paulette Holahan.

The *Adopt-A-Book Program* aims to help the University Library build its resources with the purchase of those books, audiovisual materials, sound recordings, and music scores the Library needs. By donating funds for a specific title or subject area, an individual can help the Library to better meet the teaching and research needs of Loyola's faculty and students.

If you would like to know more about the program and receive a list of titles needed by the Library, come by or call Edith Roy at **865-3346.**

## Adopt-A-Book Donors:

| | |
|---|---|
| Mrs. Janet Bean | Ms. Darla H. Rushing and |
| Dr. Elmo Cerise | Dr. Frank E. Durham |
| Mr. William F. Finegan | Mr. Leon Sarpy |
| Mr. Barry d. LeBlanc | Sisters of St. Clare's Monastary |
| Dean John J. McAulay | Mr. Oswald Sobrino |
| Dr. I. Ricardo Martinez, Jr. | Ms. Karen K. Spano |
| Ms. Deborah Poole | Mrs. A. J. Valentino |
| Mr. Robert J. Rathe | Mr. Charles W. Wall,Sr. |
| Judge William V. Redmann | |
| Mr. Nash C. Roberts, Jr. | |

## University Library Visiting Committe Members:

| | |
|---|---|
| Mr. Alexander Allain | Mrs. Rosa Keller |
| Mrs. Janet Bean | Mrs. Helen Kohlman |
| Mrs. Maedell Braud | Mrs. Verna Landrieu |
| Mrs. Florence E. Borders | Mrs. Ruth McCusker |
| Mr. and Mrs. David Dixon | Mrs. Anne Milling |
| Dr. and Mrs. Lucius Doucet, II | Dr. Walker Percy |
| Miss Ruth Dreyfous | Mrs. Cathy Pierson |
| Mrs. Mary Anna Feibelman | Mr. Nash C. Roberts, Jr. |
| Mr.Tony Gagliano | Mrs. Margie Ruli |
| Mrs. Brenda Hatfield | Dr. Jessie C. Smith |
| Mrs. Paulette Holahan | Mr. Charles W. Wall, Sr. |

# In the Media Center...

## Services

**Equipment to view or listen to:** videotapes/16mm film/laser discs/35mm slides /filmstrips/phonodiscs/audio cassette and reel to reel tapes - camcorders are also available
**Software collection:** videotapes/16mm film/laser discs/35mm slides/filmstrips/ phonodiscs/audio cassette tapes/maps
**Carrels** for viewing software in all formats
**Viewing Rooms** for small and large groups
**Interactive video stations:** Levels I, II, III
**Photographic production**
**Film rental and loan**
**Audio/video tape duplication** (some restrictions apply)
**Overhead transparencies**
**Faculty reserve section**
*LUCI* **terminal**

Equipment may be used for classes, faculty research projects, and campus activities. **Faculty and support staff are the only persons who may reserve equipment.** Students must have authorization from either a member of the faculty or support staff to use equipment for classroom presentations.

## How to order:

Come to the Media Center or call us THREE DAYS IN ADVANCE. You may also send your requests in writing (Box 152). **We are especially grateful to patrons who send requests covering the entire semester. Equipment is reserved on a "first come, first served" basis.**

## Contact:

Anne M. Ramagos, CSJ - Director
JoEva Flettrich - Film Coordinator
Dana Nixon - Equipment Supervisor
Phone x2541/2542
Miller Hall Library
Third Floor
P.O. Box 152

## Media Center Hours:
| | |
|---|---|
| Monday-Thursday | 8:30-*7:30 |
| Friday | 8:30-4:45 |
| Saturday | to be arranged |

\* *starting date will be announced*

## Faculty Carrels

A limited number of faculty carrels are available for those faculty doing research. For more information come by or call the Government Documents Department in Miller Hall Library at x2158.

## Acquisitions list available

Readers interested in receiving Loyola Library's list of new books, sound recordings, and scores, may call or write Edith Roy at extension 3346, Box 198.

# Books in Brief

McNeal, Robert H. *Stalin: Man and Ruler.* New York: New York University Press, 1988. DK268.S8 M36 1988

Few people would deny Joseph Stalin a place among the greatest leaders of history. Fewer still would deny him a place among history's greatest villains. Under his leadership the Soviet Union consolidated its revolution and transformed itself from a backward peasant society into one of the premier industrial powers of the world. He guided his country through its most severe crisis, the war with Germany that destroyed the mighty German army and defeated fascism.

Yet Stalin is known not for his triumphs but for his crimes. With quiet relentless energy he outmaneuvered his rivals and emerged triumphant after Lenin's death. His decision in 1928 to go forward with the collectivization of agriculture disrupted the countryside and resulted in a famine that claimed millions of lives. In 1937 he turned on his former comrades and launched the purges that decimated the Communist Party. He oversaw the creation of a vast system of forced labor camps populated by millions of his countrymen.

In *Stalin: Man and Ruler*, Robert H. McNeal reassesses Stalin in order to put the dictator in clearer perspective. McNeal is certainly no friend of Stalin or the Soviet Union; his aim is the historical scholar's: to gain a truer picture of the past by examining its complexity.

A case in point is McNeal's treatment of the collectivization of agriculture. In contrast to the traditional picture of Stalin as solely responsible for pushing an entire nation into murderous opposition to the hapless peasants, McNeal offers a leader pulled forward, to some degree, by the still existing revolutionary fervor of the proletariat and by genuine resentment of the peasants' economic influence.

The author shows that Stalin even moderated the zeal of those in charge of collectivization at the local level. Stalin agreed to collectivization, gave the orders which set it in motion, but was not alone in responsibility for its consequences.

McNeal's revisionism is less prominent in his treatment of the purges of the Communist Party. He sees Stalin as personally responsible for the purges, capable of commencing or stopping them at any point. But McNeal stresses the mammoth sweep of the purges, the self-perpetuating inertia that eventually threatened Stalin's power itself. Without plunging into the treacherous world of psychological history, McNeal joins numerous others in speculating that Stalin's attack against the Party was likely the product of mental imbalance. All the same, the dictator pulled back from the brink of complete madness and halted the purges.

Stalin emerges from McNeal's study as a political man who never lost sight of his ultimate goal: the creation of a socialist society in the Soviet Union. Although he exercised tremendous individual power, he was not totally free of the political and social forces which restrain any political leader. Rather than an evil genius of malevolent power, Stalin was a coldhearted realist, cynical of human foibles, yet still a visionary who moved ruthlessly toward what he believed was right for Russia. Despite his hunger for personal power, his murderous suspicions, Stalin remained a Marxist-Leninist who exerted his all to protect and continue the Bolshevik revolution.

*-Richard Snow*
*Collection Development Librarian*

---

## Who's Reading What?

**Craig Bogar,** Recreational Sports Director. *Cardinal of the Kremlin* by Tom Clancy
"About the race to develop star wars between the U.S. and the U.S.S.R...mixed with secret agents and double agents...Tom Clancy is the only one who can combine authenticity and realism as well as excitement."

**Mary Grey Hardwick,** Bookstore Manager. *The Hero Within* by Carol S. Pearson
"Carol Pearson combines literature, anthropology and psychology to clearly define the six archetypes that exist in us all--Innocent, Orphan, Wanderer, Martyr, Warrior, and Magician."

**Richard Johnson,** English Professor *Bred in the Bone* by Richardson Davies
"Another fine novel about forgery/plagiarism. Davies is a wonderful Canadian writer...his novels convey a sense of cultural change in that country over the course of the century."

**Dusty Miller,** Danna Center Director *Alaska* by James Michener
"...Covers huge expanses of time, energy and growth as almost all Michener's books do...many subplots, very historical, true Michener style."

**Jessie Nash,** History Professor *Queen of the Damned* by Anne Rice
"Mythology of the West and the old gods of Egypt..Ann Rice has a great feel for the changes in popular culture...She blends past and present very niftily and rather intriguingly."

**Cora Presley,** History Professor *Squatters and the Roots of Mau Mau, 1905-1963* by Tabitha Kanogo
"Addresses the issue of social change and nationalism..women in nationalism and peasant participation in Africa...a major contribution in these areas."

**Barbara Slifkin,** Health Services Acting Director. *Whirlwind* by James Clavall
" A grasp of not only the problems of the Iranians today, but also what will be a problem in times to come...from reading *Whirlwind* I could understand the wrenching of the garments and why it took them so long to bury Khomeini...insatiable reading."

**Gary Talarcheck,** Grants and Research Director. *Bonfire of the Vanities* by Tom Wolfe
"In the vein of his earlier pop sociology-but this time he admits it's fiction."
"...Quintessential N.Y. novel...memorable characters whom Tom Wolfe lumps all together and sparks fly."
*-Chris South*
*Government Documents Assistant*

## Notes on Business Research: *CD/Disclosure*

Need a list of some of the major plastics manufacturers in Akron, Ohio? Want current financial information on Texaco? Do you need your information quickly? CD/Disclosure (available at Loyola's Main Library) may be just what you need.

CD/Disclosure is primarily a database of reports on the more than 12,000 public companies which are required to supply information on their operations to the SEC (Securities and Exchange Commission).

The information in these reports is primarily derived from annual reports, and financial reports such as the 10-K and the 10-Q. What makes CD/Disclosure more than just a collection of reports is the powerful software included in the system to aid in searching for and downloading of the specific information you need.

### Easy Menu Searching

Using this search mode, you can begin performing profitable searches almost immediately. With Easy Menu Searching you can search for information from many different angles, including company name, type of business, geographic location, size of business (number of employees and/or volume of sales), etc.

These various access points can be used alone, or they may be used in conjunction with others to create a more specific search. Not only can you search in a number of different ways, but you can also have the system compile the information you find in many formats.

This system can provide information in a very brief form such as a company profile, or it can provide a complete report which may range up to thirty or forty pages in length. **Information can be downloaded from CD/Disclosure to a floppy disk and taken to another PC and edited there.**

If you are working with financial data, the system will also allow you to download information formatted to work with **dBase 3 or Lotus 1-2-3.**

### Dialog Emulation Searching

To get the most out of CD/Disclosure, one must eventually learn to search in Dialog Emulation mode. Dialog Emulation Searching, which has nearly all the characteristics of searching an online database, can do everything Easy Menu Searching can do and a lot more. You may search by keyword, and every report in which your term appears will be pulled up. You may also combine terms using the boolean operators "and", "or", and "not" to make your search more or less inclusive.

First-time users of CD/Disclosure Easy Menu Mode or Dialog Emulation Searching are strongly advised to consult with a Reference Librarian before beginning to ensure that your experiences with this system are enjoyable and productive.
*-Mark Sutton*
*Head of Reference*

## Recently Received Gifts

*Thank you!*

*On behalf of the students and faculty, the Library would like to thank the following individuals and organizations for their donations and continued interest in the Library:*

| | |
|---|---|
| Professor Jessie Barfield | Archives/Special Collections |
| Professor Richard W. Bevis and Professor Marcus Smith | Books *(In memory of Peter Kilburn)* |
| Mr. Howard Brehm | Sound Recordings |
| Mr. Joseph W. Browning | Books |
| Rev. Thomas H. Clancey, SJ | Books |
| Mr. John M. Coates | Sound Recordings |
| Professor Ted Cotton | Books |
| Mrs. Denning | Books |
| Mrs. Mary Dixon | Sound Recordings |
| Professor Barbara Ewell | Books |
| Mr. and Mrs. Randy Florent | Funds *(In memory of Hester B. Slocum)* |
| Mrs. Betty Fosberg | Funds *(In memory of Wallace Leftwich)* |
| Professor Bill Huey | Books |
| Sister Fara Impastato | Books |
| Professor Jake Jacobs | Periodicals |
| Professor Edward Kvet | Books/Music |

| | |
|---|---|
| Dr. Mark McKnight | Books/Music |
| Mrs. Gloria L. Mouledoux | Archives/Special Coll. |
| Professor Earl Richard and Dr. Mary Ann Richter | Books |
| Mr. O. Jack Schneidau | Funds |
| Mr. Eric Scholl | Books |
| Father Youree Watson, SJ | Books |
| Professor Xenia Zeldin | Books/Microforms |

## Gifts Welcomed

All Friends of the Library are encouraged to make donations of books, periodicals, or other materials to our collection. Anyone interested in making donations may call Richard Snow (books) or Rosalee McReynolds (periodicals) at 865-3346, Art Carpenter (archives/special collections) at 865-3186, Sister Annie Ramagos (audiovisual/media) at 865-2541, or Laura Dankner (music) at 865-2774.

With each cash donation of $25.00 or more, the donor and person in whose name the gift is made will be acknowledged with a bookplate.

## Hints for Using *LUCI:*
## *Searching by publisher*
*(Note: This will be much more meaningful if you are sitting at a terminal.)*

One of the little known features of *LUCI* is that the system can be searched by publisher. This is a helpful search key if you are interested in what the Library owns by a particular publisher, or if you can't remember the exact title but you know the name of the publisher. It is also useful to some degree in searching regional subjects in that you can, for example, search Louisiana State University Press.

### *How it's done:*

To do a publisher search you need to search in "ALL CATEGORIES" and use the KEYWORD option. In response to the prompt, "TYPE SEARCH WORD(S)," you might type in "260=LOUISIANA STATE UNIVERSITY PRESS." (260 is the code that identifies publishers.) Then press KEYWORD.

At this writing we have 798 titles in the database published by LSU press. Obviously, this is a case where you would most likely want to further limit your search. There follow two examples of search refinement, one limiting the search to a topic and the other limiting the search by type of material.

### *Searching publisher and subject:*

A search for "260=NORTON" retrieves 1065 listings. In order to see only our music holdings published by Norton you might try this search:

Choose "ALL CATEGORIES," and then respond to the prompt, "TYPE TITLE WORD(S)," by typing in "MUSIC AND 260=NORTON," then press KEYWORD.

This search, which looks for the word "music" in all author, title, and subject fields should find all materials that we own having anything to do with music and published by Norton. There are 118 such listings at this time.

When you are doing a comprehensive search like this, be sure to type in the topic word or words first. **If you type in "260=NORTON AND MUSIC" the computer thinks you are looking for a publisher whose name is "Norton and Music."**

### *Searching publisher and format:*

A search for "260=TIME LIFE" retrieves, at this writing, 133 responses, including books, records, and AV material. If you want to look at only AV material published by Time-Life, you can refine your search by starting over and typing in "260=TIME LIFE AND F=AVM" (format=audiovisual material), then press KEYWORD; or you could use your first response from "260=TIMELIFE" on the SEARCH HISTORY screen, press the COMPOSE key, and then type "1" (meaning 260=TIME LIFE) "AND F=AVM." You will see that we have 77 entries for AV materials published by Time-Life.

### *I know the publisher but I can't quite remember the title...*

An example of how the publisher search can help when you "sort of" remember the title can be illustrated this way: You think the title contains the words "human behavior" or "social behavior" and you know that the publisher is Elsevier.

Choose "ALL CATEGORIES" again and type in "HUMAN BEHAVIOR OR SOCIAL BEHAVIOR AND 260= ELSEVIER," then press KEYWORD. this search key will retrieve 5 responses, including the book you are looking for, *The Evolution of Human Social Behavior.*

The publisher search is a good short cut in a case such as this. Otherwise, the search for only "HUMAN BEHAVIOR OR SOCIAL BEHAVIOR" without the "AND=ELSEVIER" retrieves 213 responses which you would have to wade through to find your title.

At the present time a publisher search cannot be combined with a call number search, but we are hoping to add this feature at a later time, as this would be particularly helpful for searching literature topics.

*-Darla Rushing*
*Head of Cataloging*

## LOYOLA
### NEW ORLEANS
Loyola University Library
6363 St. Charles Avenue, Box 198
New Orleans, Lousiana 70118

# *Library Newsletter*

## Elizabeth Coates Maddux Library
## Trinity University

Format: stapled

Size: 8 1/2 by 11"

Color: buff

Number of pages: varies

Frequency: annually

Cost: n.a.

Number of copies: 300 - 500

Audience: faculty, staff, and administration

Editorial responsibility: permanent editor; library director

Desktop software: n.a.

**Issue Number Two**                                              **Spring 1989**

# LIBRARY NEWSLETTER
## ELIZABETH COATES MADDUX LIBRARY
## TRINITY UNIVERSITY

---

## INTERLIBRARY LOAN (ILL)

Interlibrary loan has become increasingly popular with students and faculty as research interests have expanded. We will obtain over 50% more items for our users this year than we did for the 1986-87 year. ILL staff are also working on ways to expedite the delivery of items our users receive from other libraries. A fax machine, purchased expressly for ILL use, enables us to receive many items much more quickly than mail allows. In addition to the special arrangement with the University of Texas at Austin, during the past year we also set up an expedited resource sharing pilot program with Baylor University, Southern Methodist University, and Texas Christian University.

Chris Nolan

\* \* \* \* \*

## SUMMER LIBRARY HOURS

Library hours during the summer will change, as usual. Watch the signs posted on the front door or call the library hours number at x8126.

## INVENTORY CLOSING

The Library will be closed August 7-18 for inventory. During this time, access to the Library will be provided for Trinity students, faculty, and staff, upon request. Please call extension x8121 if you need access to the Library during those weeks.

## BIBLIOGRAPHIC INSTRUCTION

Liaison librarians work with faculty to provide bibliographic instruction for classes working on assignments that require Library use. The librarian will generally make a presentation to the class and prepare appropriate bibliographies or other materials. Students are then able to make appointments for individual consultations with the librarian following the presentation.

More than sixty sessions per year are presented. Student evaluations have indicated that they are very helpful.

Contact your liaison librarian if you would like to request a presentation for your classes.

Barbara Ford

\* \* \* \* \*

## FIRST YEAR SEMINARS

Reference librarians will continue to work with faculty teaching the First Year Seminar to enhance students' bibliographic skills. During the workshop in May, librarians will make a presentation for those teaching the seminars, and bibliographies and other aids will be distributed. Librarians are also available to make classroom presentations upon request.

BF

## EXPANDED TABLE OF CONTENTS SERVICE

In the fall of 1988 the Maddux Library initiated an expanded serials table of contents service for Trinity faculty members. For several years we had been providing table of contents service for serials to which the Library subscribes. The new service offers faculty the opportunity to review tables of contents pages for serials to which we do not subscribe.

The expanded service is provided by using Current Contents, published weekly by the Institute for Scientific Information in seven separate discipline-oriented editions. The Library subscribes to five sections which are appropriate to our curriculum: Arts & Humanities; Social & Behavioral Sciences; Engineering, Technology, and Applied Science; Life Sciences; and Physical, Chemical and Earth Sciences. The issues reproduce the tables of contents of journals and other serials in each subject area.

Faculty members desiring this service may submit up to five titles each for which they would like to receive table of contents pages. The requests of several faculty members within a department may be coordinated. At this time the Library is serving twelve departments with table of contents pages for fifty-seven different titles.

Faculty members who are interested in this expanded table of contents service or who have any questions about it should contact their liaison librarian.

Kathryn Soupiset

## EXHIBITS OF NEW ACQUISITIONS

Two sources served as the basis for the library exhibit of January-March 1989: Notable Medical Books from the Lilly Library, Indiana University, prepared by William R. Le Fanu, Emeritus Librarian, Royal College of Surgeons of England, London, published by the Lilly Research Laboratories, Indianapolis, 1976; and The Classics of Surgery Library, published by Gryphon Editions, Ltd., Birmingham, Alabama.

The medical books in the exhibit, selected from the Ziperman Collection donated to Trinity University in December 1988 by Mrs. H. Haskell Ziperman in memory of her husband, Colonel H. Haskell Ziperman, made some contribution to the increase of knowledge or the advancement of medical care.

These twenty-one volumes sampled great discoveries as recorded by those who made them. A brief account of each writer's life and his work and an historical framework for his contribution to medical knowledge were provided.

The current exhibit, which will be on display from April through June, consists of selections from the Ziperman Postcard Collection, which contains over 23,000 postcards presented to the university by the same donor noted above. The exhibits, located on Levels 2, 3, and 4, feature colored picture postcards from Indonesia, Japan, Korea, and the People's Republic of China. Deltiologists, collectors of postcards, can take vicarious trips around the world simply by flipping through their cards, and with a sense of pleasure, mail them from the Great Wall of China, or the temples of Seoul, or the lovely countryside of Japan and exclaim, "Look where I am."

Katherine Pettit

## CAMPUS WIRED FOR CABLE TV

After several years of negotiations, the campus has now been wired for cable television. As you may know, the cable TV franchise agreement with the City of San Antonio requires the franchise holder to install one cable outlet and provide basic service to each classroom building and dormitory on campus at no charge to the University. Basic service includes:

Local television stations and PBS;
C-SPAN (the Congressional sessions and the local government channel);
Cable News Network;
Local access channels;
Spanish language channels;
Health channel;
New York and American Stock Exchange channel;
New York, Chicago, and Atlanta stations;
several other channels.

In addition, the campus has the potential of being wired so that programs

originating at the Library or communications center can be transmitted to most of the academic buildings on campus. This will make it feasible to show a video tape to a class by playing the tape in the Library and transmitting it through the cable to the classroom. Thus for any room with a cable outlet and a television set, this system could eliminate the need to transport video tape equipment. The program would be available only through our campus system.

These classrooms have cable outlets:

Chapman Graduate Center Room 105 & 410
Cowles Life Science - (system)
Halsell Administrative Center - 342
Marrs McLean Science Center - 170
Parker Chapel - 106
Richardson Communication Center - (all)
Science Lecture Hall
Storch Education Center - 109
Holt Center - 300
Ruth Taylor Art - 217
Ruth Taylor Theatre - 208
Moody Engineering Science - 105
Maddux Library - (system)

At work at a fifteenth-century printing press. Reproduced from the cover of the Journal of the American Society for Information Science (July 1987, v. 38, no. 4).

## LCD COMPUTER PROJECTION PANEL

A new service now available through IMS makes it possible to project the image from a computer onto a standard projection screen. A special liquid crystal display (LCD) is connected to the output of the computer and uses the light from an overhead projector to display the image. This enlarged display allows an entire class to view the output of the computer.

The size of the projected image is limited only by the screen size and the distance of the overhead from the screen. The LCD will work with IBM PS/2, IBM PC XT/AT and compatibles, and MacIntosh Plus and SE computers with a video output. The Sharp QA-50 projection panel is a monochrome (black and white) display; however, colors can be represented by eight shades of grey.

Please call IMS for more information on compatibility and availability.

Ronnie Swanner

## AUTOMATED SERVICES

### PUBLIC OCLC TERMINAL

An OCLC (Online Computer Library Center) terminal for public use has been installed in the reference area. Library users are now able to have access to the holdings of more than 3,000 libraries. This terminal has been helpful in identifying libraries from which materials can be obtained on interlibrary loan and it also facilitates bibliographic verification and reference work.

BF

\* \* \* \* \*

### INTEGRATED SYSTEMS

Over the past several years, members of the Library Activities Committee, Library and computer center staff, and campus community have seen demonstrations from several vendors of integrated online systems for library catalogs. We continue to monitor developments. Interest in these systems has increased as they have become more sophisticated and provide expanded means to obtain access to library holdings and are available in a number of academic libraries.

BF

\* \* \* \* \*

### ONLINE SEARCHING

Maddux Library's online searching program has continued to grow over the past year. We now provide searching in the evening on so-called "after hours services," BRS After Dark and Knowledge Index. These provide access to many of the most popular databases available during the daytime, but with a significant reduction in cost. For example, INSPEC, a popular physics, engineering, and computer science database, costs over $100 per search hour during the day, but only $18 at night. Also, the Library will pay the first $5.00 of one search per semester for all faculty and students. Since the nighttime databases are so cheap, many students and faculty who have had searches done then have in effect gotten free searches. During the fall semester, the reference librarians did searching two nights per week; during the spring we expanded to three nights. We plan to continue offering the service next fall.

Sallie Barringer

## SDI (SELECTIVE DISSEMINATION OF INFORMATION)

Another online service that is less well known is SDI (Selective Dissemination of Information). For an SDI, you set up a basic search on a particular topic in a particular database. As the database is updated, the search is automatically run against the most recent additions to the database, and you are mailed the results. This is an inexpensive ($5.00 - $12.00 per month), easy way to stay up with current research in an area in which you are working. If you would like to begin an SDI, call your liaison librarian.

SB

\* \* \* \* \*

### CD-ROM (COMPACT DISK--READ ONLY MEMORY)

In addition to providing remote access to databases, we are investigating the possibility of acquiring the databases themselves. A number of popular databases are now available on CD-ROM (Compact Disk--Read Only Memory). With the CD-ROM version of a particular database, users can have unlimited searching with no hourly or citation charges. We currently have one CD-ROM database, the Corporate and Industry Research Reports (CIRR), a collection of business and financial reports on various companies, produced by accounting and investment firms. If you would like more information on CD-ROM, please contact your liaison librarian.

SB

\* \* \* \* \*

### NEW REFERENCE TOOLS

New reference sets in the Maddux Library include International Encyclopedia of Communications (REF P 87.5 I5); the Encyclopedia of Asian History (REF DS 31 E53); Worldmark Encyclopedia of Nations, 1988 edition (REF G 63 W67); and the New Grove Dictionary of Jazz (REF ML 102 J3 N48). Several other new titles which will be published over many years have started arriving: Allgemeines Kunstler-Lexicon (REF N 40 A63); Encyclopedia of Architecture: Design, Engineering, and Construction (REF NA 31 E59); and the Encyclopedia of Mathematics (REF QA 5 M3713). The second edition of the Oxford English Dictionary has been ordered and will likely be made available this summer.

Craig Likness

## EXTENDED BORROWING FOR STUDENTS

In response to requests from faculty and students, and since students are occasionally involved in research projects which require extended use of certain Library books, the Library now provides for selected students an opportunity to borrow books for a semester. A special Library form, signed by any faculty member, allows that student to borrow materials on an extended loan. The form is valid for an entire semester and must be presented each time books are needed for a circulation period longer than the usual three weeks. Copies of the form are available at the circulation desk.

Mary Clarkson

* * * * *

## NEW FACULTY ORIENTATION

During the orientation held for new faculty in the fall, Robert Blystone, John Donahue, and Charles Talbot made presentations concerning bibliographic instruction.

The presentations were well received by the new faculty and led to several requests for course-integrated bibliographic instruction. These activities will be continued in the fall as we work to expand our bibliographic instruction efforts.

BF

* * * * *

## LIBRARY GUIDES

Each year new printed guides are added to the selection available in the Reference Department. Please let us know if there are any additional printed aids you think might be useful to have available.

SOME PEER INSTITUTION COMPARISONS, 1987-88

TABLE I.
Holdings, Books & Bound Periodicals
   as of July 1988--Top 20

| | | |
|---|---|---|
| 1 | Smith | 1,013,385 * |
| 2 | Oberlin | 969,056 |
| 3 | Wesleyan | 938,759 |
| 4 | Trinity, Conn. | 778,092 * |
| 5 | Bowdoin | 727,663 * |
| 6 | Bryn Mawr | 711,082 |
| 7 | Amherst | 684,172 |
| 8 | Vassar | 655,361 |
| 9 | Williams | 643,473 |
| 10 | Wellesley | 632,418 |
| 11 | TRINITY UNIV. | 619,222 |
| 12 | Mt. Holyoke | 546,206 |
| 13 | Swarthmore | 529,231 |
| 14 | Bucknell | 483,263 |
| 15 | Occidental | 478,507 |
| 16 | Colgate | 439,079 |
| 17 | Hamilton | 432,263 * |
| 18 | Connecticut College | 424,815 |
| 19 | Carleton | 419,538 |
| 20 | Middlebury | 399,439 |

\* Includes government
   documents

TABLE II.
Library expenditures per student--
   Top 20

| | | |
|---|---|---|
| 1 | Amherst | $1,315 |
| 2 | Swarthmore | $1,306 |
| 3 | TRINITY with IMS | $1,237 |
| 4 | Bryn Mawr | $1,213 |
| 5 | TRINITY without IMS | $1,149 |
| 6 | Haverford | $1,130 |
| 7 | Bowdoin | $1,110 |
| 8 | Univ. of the South | $1,061 |
| 9 | Oberlin | $1,039 |
| 10 | Vassar | $1,017 |
| 11 | Grinnell | $1,016 |
| 12 | Hamilton | $990 |
| 13 | Smith | $986 |
| 14 | Wellesley | $961 |
| 15 | Middlebury | $941 |
| 16 | Occidental | $939 |
| 17 | Trinity, Conn. | $894 |
| 18 | Mt. Holyoke | $884 |
| 19 | Wesleyan | $842 |
| 20 | Davidson | $809 |

TABLE III.
Library Expenditures as
   Percentage of Education and
   General Budget (E&G)--Top 21

| | | |
|---|---|---|
| 1 | TRINITY with IMS | 8.2% |
| 2 | TRINITY without IMS | 7.7% |
| 3 | Amherst | 6.7% |
| 4 | Haverford | 6.7% |
| 5 | Occidental | 6.3% |
| 6 | Smith | 6.2% |
| 7 | Drew | 6.2% * |
| 8 | Bryn Mawr | 6.1% |
| 9 | Carleton | 6.1% |
| 10 | Vassar | 6.1% |
| 11 | Oberlin | 5.6% |
| 12 | Trinity, Conn. | 5.5% |
| 13 | Wellesley | 5.4% |
| 14 | Univ. of the South | 5.4% |
| 15 | Grinnell | 5.3% |
| 16 | Middlebury | 5.2% |
| 17 | Hamilton | 5.2% |
| 18 | Wesleyan | 5.1% |
| 19 | Swarthmore | 5.1% |
| 20 | Connecticut College | 5.1% |
| 21 | Davidson | 5.0% |

\* '86-'87 data

TABLE IV.
Acquisitions Expenditures--Top 19

| | | |
|---|---|---|
| 1 | TRINITY with IMS | $1,277,215 |
| 2 | TRINITY without IMS | $1,257,373 |
| 3 | Smith | $1,008,198 |
| 4 | Vassar | $975,779 |
| 5 | Wesleyan | $938,850 |
| 6 | Oberlin | $828,466 |
| 7 | Bucknell | $818,088 |
| 8 | Amherst | $786,351 |
| 9 | Hamilton | $773,810 |
| 10 | Bryn Mawr | $768,314 |
| 11 | Wellesley | $735,140 |
| 12 | Colgate | $727,293 |
| 13 | Williams | $695,258 |
| 14 | Bowdoin | $691,835 |
| 15 | Occidental | $691,176 |
| 16 | Middlebury | $676,966 |
| 17 | Swarthmore | $653,892 |
| 18 | Carleton | $630,688 |
| 19 | Trinity, Conn. | $618,241 |

SOME RECOMMENDATIONS FOR SUMMER READING FROM THE BROWSING COLLECTION

Paul Monette. BORROWED TIME. AN AIDS MEMOIR. (Browsing RC 607 A26 M66)

This personal documentary about Monette and his friend, Roger Horwitz, who died from AIDS related disease, stands as a remarkable autobiography. Moreover, it is a truly moving and superbly written book about how AIDS is devastating lives of those around us.

McGeorge Bundy. DANGER AND SURVIVAL. CHOICES ABOUT THE BOMB IN THE FIRST FIFTY YEARS. (Browsing UA 23 B786)

Reviewers are recognizing this book as the most comprehensive political history of the nuclear bomb yet written. Bundy gives particular attention to Khrushchev's challenges in Berlin and the Cuban missile crisis.

Strobe Talbott. THE MASTER OF THE GAME. PAUL NITZE AND THE NUCLEAR PEACE. (Browsing JX 1974.7 T264)

If you make it through Bundy, Talbott will supplement your effort with his assessment of the forty years of U.S. and Soviet discussion on reducing nuclear weapons. Talbott was a Rhodes Scholar and is now Washington Bureau Chief for Time.

Francois Jacob. THE STATUE WITHIN. (Browsing QH 429.2 J33 A313)

This publication, the memoirs of France's notable molecular biologist, stands as another recent outstanding autobiography. Jacob shared the 1965 Nobel Prize for Medicine.

Michael P. Cohen. THE HISTORY OF THE SIERRA CLUB 1892-1970. (Browsing QH 76 C64)

Here's a massive tome to take with you on your Western states camping trip. The author has published other books on John Muir. He is a Sierra Club "insider."

Robert Wright. THREE SCIENTISTS AND THEIR GODS. LOOKING FOR INFORMATION IN AN AGE OF INFORMATION. (Browsing Q 360 W75)

The publishers describe this work as an intellectual adventure story, both scientific and spiritual. At the center are Ed Fredkin, E.O. Wilson, and Kenneth Boulding.

Neil Baldwin. MAN RAY. AMERICAN ARTIST. (Browsing N 6537 R3 B3)

First biography of this painter, sculptor, filmmaker, printmaker, objectmaker, collagist, photographer, poet, essayist, philosopher, and gadfly. Famous quote from Man Ray: "I photograph what you can't paint, and I paint what you can't photograph."

Ned Rorem. SETTLING THE SCORE. ESSAYS ON MUSIC. (Browsing ML 60 R7845)

Reflecting the author's iconoclastic views on contemporary music, these brief essays are wonderfully written examples of the genre. Full of bite as well as insight.

John Boswell. THE KINDNESS OF STRANGERS. THE ABANDONMENT OF CHILDREN IN WESTERN EUROPE FROM LATE ANTIQUITY TO THE RENAISSANCE. (Browsing HV 887 E8 B67)

Social history at its most fascinating. Boswell uses civil and canon law, trial records, foundling-hospital archives, and art in this study which is likely to be controversial. He is a professor of history at Yale.

Diane Gentry. ENDURING WOMEN. (Browsing HQ 1412 G46)

The author/photographer's personal look into the lives of ten American women who are far removed from the media's vision of the successful woman. A wonderful book by a San Antonio author.

Leonard W. Levy. ORIGINAL INTENT AND THE FRAMERS' CONSTITUTION. (Browsing KF 4550 L48)

The New York Times considers this one of the most important books of the year. The author, a noted constitutional scholar, evaluates the doctrine of original intent by examining sources of constitutional law and landmark cases.

Hedrick Smith. THE POWER GAME. HOW WASHINGTON WORKS. (Browsing JK 271 S577)

If you really want to know, this author will reveal how Washington works from the inside. He is a former Washington correspondent of The New York Times and a Pulitzer Prize winner.

John D'Emilio and Estelle Freedman. INTIMATE MATTERS. A HISTORY OF SEXUALITY IN AMERICA. (Browsing HQ 18 U5 D45)

This unique study by two young social/family historians is very well written as well as exemplary historical research from a feminist perspective.

Elizabeth Abbott. HAITI. THE DUVALIERS AND THEIR LEGACY. (Browsing F 1928 A583)

The "shocking" inside story is based primarily on interviews with Haitians. The author is an historian and journalist. Don't travel there this summer; read the book instead.

Said Amir Abjomand. THE TURBAN FOR THE CROWN. THE ISLAMIC REVOLUTION IN IRAN. (Browsing DS 316.6 A74)

Of the many new books on this subject, this one is getting the most enthusiastic reviews.

Yehoshafat Harkabi. ISRAEL'S FATEFUL HOUR. (Browsing DS 126.5 H357213)

This book presents a powerful argument for Israeli negotiation with the Arabs by an Israeli who was an advisor to Menachem Begin. Very controversial.

Marie Brenner. HOUSE OF DREAMS. THE BINGHAM FAMILY OF LOUISVILLE. (Browsing CT 274 B52 B74)

One of several new books on a fascinating American family. All the elements of "compelling" fiction are here. Brenner was born in San Antonio and visits the city on occasion. Recently she irritated Henry Cisneros with a feature in Vanity Fair.


NEW FICTION SET IN EXOTIC PLACES


Aldo Busi. THE STANDARD LIFE OF A TEMPORARY PANTYHOSE SALESMAN. (Italy) (Browsing PQ 4862 U824 V5813)

Isabel Allende. EVA LUNA. (Chile) (Browsing PQ 8098.1 L54 E813)

Penelope Lively. MOON TIGER. (London/the World) (Winner of the Booker Prize) (Browsing PR 6062 I 89 M66)

Paul West. THE PLACE IN FLOWERS WHERE POLLEN RESTS. (Hopi mesas of Arizona) (Browsing PR 6073 E766 P55)

Janet Frame. THE CARPATHIANS. (New Zealand) (Browsing PR 9639.3 F7 C3)

Rodney Hall. KISSES OF THE ENEMY. (Australia) (Browsing PR 9619.3 H285 K57)

Edward Abbey. THE FOOL'S PROGRESS. (From Arizona to West Virginia) (Browsing PS 3551 B2 F6)

Kate Braverman. PALM LATITUDES. (Barrio of Los Angeles) (Browsing PS 355 2 R3555 P35)

Vicki Covington. GATHERING HOME. (Alabama) (Browsing PS 3553 0883 G37)

Kathryn Davis. LABRADOR. (No, not Canada, rather New Hampshire) (Browsing PS 3554 A934924 L3)

Gretel Ehrlich. HEART MOUNTAIN. (Wyoming) (Browsing PS 3555 H72 H4)

Jonathan Franzen. THE TWENTY-SEVENTH CITY. (St. Louis) (Browsing PS 3556 R352 T8)

Judith Grossman. HER OWN TERMS. (Oxford) (Browsing PS 3557 R6724 H47)

Cecelia Holland. THE LORDS OF VAUMARTIN. (Medieval Paris)
(Browsing PS 3558 O348 L67)

Dan O'Brien. SPIRIT OF THE HILLS. (Black Hills of South Dakota)
(Browsing PS 3565 B665 S65)

Tova Reich. THE MASTER OF RETURN. (Jerusalem) (Browsing PS 3568 E4763 M37)

W. T. Tyler. THE LION AND THE JACKAL. (Africa) (Browsing PS 3570 Y53 L5)

Marianne Wiggins. JOHN DOLLAR. (Burma) (Browsing PS 3573 I385 J64)

Elfriede Selenek. THE PIANO TEACHER. (Vienna) (Browsing PT 2670 E46 K513)


For additional selections, remember that there are approximately 1000 new books
available for three-week circulation in the Browsing Collection (located on the
Library's lower level) at any one time.

Craig Likness

# *News from the Hill*

## Jim Dan Hill Library and Media Resource Center
## University of Wisconsin - Superior

Format:  stapled

Size:  8 1/2 by 11"

Color:  buff

Number of pages:  1 - 4

Frequency:  quarterly

Annual cost:  $0 - 500

Number of copies:  150 - 300

Audience:  faculty, staff, and administration

Editorial responsibility:  permanent editorial board; professional librarians

Desktop software:  PFS:First Publisher

# News from The Hill
### Newsletter of the Jim Dan Hill Library and Media Resource Center

## LIBRARY CHANGES

Come check out our new look! The new year brought a variety of changes to the Library. Not only has carpet been installed, but the painters have been busy brightening up some of the walls in the building.

You will also find that some of the furniture, collections, and other library accoutrements have been moved in the process. For example, the newspapers are all now available for access in the browsing room and, we have taken the current newspapers off the poles to make use easier. The card catalogs have been moved to the rear of the library to make room for the new online catalog. The cards are still available; you just have to walk a few more feet to get to them. Finally, we have continued our move to place all media-related equipment and materials on the second floor. Please ask for assistance in locating these items.

We are very excited about our most recent changes and the improved service we can now provide.

## LS/2000 IS NOW AVAILABLE!!

The new online catalog, although not complete, is available to the public at four terminasl located to your right as you enter the Library building. The system is designed to be user-friendly and includes many instructions, but we are more than happy to answer any questions faculty, staff, and students may have.

The system provides access to the collection by author, title, subject, and a variety of other searches including language, non-book materials, age level, and keyword.

Currently the database lacks all materials purchased during the past year, but these items will be added before the end of the semester. We plan to begin checking out books using the computer at that time. (You can still get a new campus ID with a barcode at the Media Resource Center.)

If you are interested in learning more about the catalog or would like a hands-on introductory session, call Kristi (x233) or any of the library faculty.

## UWS JOINS PBS SATELLITE SERVICE

UW-Extension has purchased a two year membership in the PBS Adult-Learning Satellite Service (ALSS) for ten four-year campuses and four two-year campuses in Wisconsin. UWS is one of the campuses included in the membership. ALSS distributes some teleconferences free to its members, and others for a reduced fee to non-members.

In addition to specialized teleconferences, college level telecourses are distributed by ALSS. The attached ALSS schedule should give you a good idea of what is available. The telecourses are designed for broadcast or videotape use by students, and generally have complete packaged materials including text, exams, and instructor's guides.

UWS has a collection of telecourses on videotape as a result of its participation in the CPB/Annenberg college telecourse project from 1986 to 1988. This collction is housed in Jim Dan Hill Library.

If you are interested in utilizing ALSS teleconferences, ALSS telecourses, or the Annenberg telecourses, contact Peter Nordgren at Media Resources, x340.

## ACCESS TO LACROSSE HOLDINGS

Add UW-LaCrosse to your list of campus libraries whose on-line catalogs can be accessed via micro-computer and modem. Other libraries with holdings available are Madison, Milwaukee, Eau Claire, Green Bay, and Platteville. Call x233 for assistance.

---

**News from The Hill**                                                            2

---

### BOOK REVIEW--VISION QUEST by TERRY DAVIS
### by Denise Johnson

Author Terry Davis visited UWS on Thursday, February 23rd to discuss his work for the benefit of Bob Carmack's Adolescent Literature class. In light of Mr. Davis's visit, I thought it would be fun to read and review his popular, young adult novel, *Vision Quest.* I was particularly interested in reading the novel, because it had been the focus of considerable controversy and censorship. Naturally, I wanted to know what all the fuss was about.

The book is essentially a coming-of-age novel in the tradition of *Catcher in the Rye.* The novel's protagonist, Louden Swain, is a star of his high school's wrestling team and is a thoughtful and intelligent young man groping with life's meaning. The controversy surrounding the book is undoubtingly due to its frank sexuality and realistic language. Given the time novel's setting, I would say the sexuality and language are, if anything, understated. Today's moral climate, however, is less forgiving of tender and open sexuality between young people. Even at the time the book was written, one reviewer stated, "People who don't like Judy Blume's *Forever* because of its sex-without-punishment attitude will be appalled at *Vision Quest* because it is sex not only without punishment, but with reward." (Davidson, Dave, et. al. *English Journal,* May 1980, p.92)

Focusing so much attention on the sexual situations in this novel, however interesting, is unfair to a finely written book with exceptional characterizations. Louden, his father, his girlfriend Carla, his friends on the wrestling team, even his absent mother are all fully three-dimensional characters. The usual cardboard parents and teachers in young adult novels are missing in this example of the genre. While the situations presented are not always entirely realistic, the characters are so believable and generally likeable that the unlikelihood of their living arrangement can easily be overlooked.

Terry Davis has done something more here than present an assemblage of likeable characters. His coming-of-age novel took a new approach to what has become a standardized and formulaic genre. He used Louden's preparation for the big wrestling match as an allegory for the "vision quest" (a native American coming-of-age ritual.) In doing so, he gave his novel a focus and tightness amounting almost to distillation. I couldn't put it down.

### APRIL 15TH - COMING SOON

The National Education Association Federal Income Tax Guide for Eductional Employees, 1989 edition, for 1988 taxes is now available in the library. The call number is REF KF 6369.8.E3N3 1988.

Wisconsin, Minnesota, and Federal Tax Forms and materials are available in the library, and shelved at the Public Services Desk. A videotape and audio cassette are available for assistance in filing federal tax forms. The tapes can be checked out at the Reserve Station.

### 22 THINGS TO DO IN THE JIM DAN HILL LIBRARY

Read a newspaper
Do a computer search
Take a nap
Use an out-of-town telephone book
Check out a book
Watch other people read
Find out if Pooh caught his Heffalump
Learn the warning signs for a heart attack
Tell the librarian to subscribe to more periodicals on
   Africa
Smile at the librarians
Pick up income tax forms
Meet with your friends
Find a date
Look up sample resume
Page through the latest issue of Variety
Count the number of cards in the card catalog
Direct someone to the washroom
Use the CD-ROM
Get President Shaw's address
Find out who is in the Hockey Hall of Fame
Admire the new carpet

### THE BOOK SALE IS BACK

As part of its celebration of National Library Week, the Library will hold a book sale on Thursday and Friday, April 13-14 from 9:30 AM to 3:30 PM. The sale will be held on the second floor of the library in the former EMC area. Also, watch for our Name-That-System contest to be held in April.

# *West Liberty Library Notes*

## Paul N. Elbin Library
## West Liberty State College

Format:  single sheet

Size:  8 1/2 by 11"

Color:  white

Number of pages:  2

Frequency:  quarterly

Annual cost:  $0 - 500

Number of copies:  150 - 300

Audience:  faculty, staff, administration, students, and friends

Editorial responsibility:  permanent editor; professional librarian

Desktop software:  nameplate - Newsroom; text - Word Perfect 5.0

# West Liberty
# L I B R A R Y
# N O T E S

A quarterly newsletter of the Paul N. Elbin Library,
West Liberty State College

Volume 1, Number 1                    September, 1989

## LIBRARY EARNS AN "A" ACCORDING TO COLLEGE LIBRARY STANDARDS

Acccording to national standards established by the Association of College and Research Libraries (ACRL), the Elbin Library earns the grade of "A" in each of three categories: the size of its collection, the number of staff, and the use of the space within its facilities.

Based upon the 1986 revision of ACRL's "Standards for College Libraries," a library at an instituition of the size of West Liberty (see Standards, p. 2)

## REGULAR HOURS RESUME

With the return of students to campus for the fall semester, the Elbin Library has resumed its regular schedule. Through December 14 the library will be open normally during the following hours:

| | |
|---|---|
| Monday-Thursday: | 8 AM-10 PM |
| Friday: | 8 AM- 4 PM |
| Saturday: | 10 AM- 4 PM |
| Sunday: | 2 PM-10 PM |

This issue introduces "West Liberty Library Notes," a quarterly newsletter highlighting the people and activities of the Paul N. Elbin Library. To be published concurrently with the library's accession list, the newsletter will be issued in September, December, March, and June.

## INTERLIBRARY LOAN FALL FOCUS

Unknown to most library users, the library's reach extends beyond the building that houses its collection. Through interlibrary loan, the library can tap the resources of other libraries to borrow materials for its users.

To increase patrons' awareness that there is "more to the library than the eye can see," the Elbin Library is paying tribute to interlibrary lending this fall with a variety of promotional materials. This awareness campaign is part of a larger celebration sponsored by the Online Computer Library Center (OCLC) to mark the tenth anniversary of its electronic interlibrary loan network, which serves 3,600 libraries in 26 countries.

With the rising costs of materials and services, a library often cannot purchase everything it needs to develop its collection in all areas. "Interlibrary loan allows us to make the best use of our library dollars by purchasing materials of interest to many users and borrowing single or low-demand items upon request," said Jennifer Cross, who coordinates interlibrary loan at Elbin Library. "We welcome the opportunity to (see Interlibrary Loan, p. 2)

## NEW STAFF AT LIBRARY

During the summer the Elbin Library staff welcomed two new members to their ranks. Joining the library as a Library Technical Assistant I in the sound recordings section is Alan Ramsey. He replaces Mrs. Constance Hein, who retired in June.

Alan was graduated from Berea College with a bachelor's degree in history. While at Berea he worked as an assistant in the library's circulation department. Since receiving his degree, he has been involved with the business which his family owns and operates.

John Allen Shearer, Jr., has assumed the post of Acquisitions Librarian. Originally from Pennsylvania, he has spent the last eight years in Connecticut, where he served as assistant reference librarian and head of database searching at Central Connecticut State University. He holds a bachelor's degree in English from Westminster College and a master's degree in library science from the University of Pittsburgh. He has done additional graduate study at Trinity College as well.

## STANDARDS (cont.)

should have a collection of about 167,000 volumes, whereas the Elbin Library's collection actually contains over 199,000 volumes. Similarly, the standards recommend a staff of five librarians, while the WLSC library has 4.5 professional positions. Finally, the Elbin Library's 46,200 square feet of "net assignable area" exceeds the 39,000 square feet that the ACRL guidelines advocate.

These statistics were compiled recently at the request of the statewide Library Resources Advisory Council (LRAC).

## INTERLIBRARY LOAN (cont.)

extend this valuable service to our users."

For more information on the library's interlibrary loan services, visit the library or call 336-8035.

## FRIENDS OF THE LIBRARY GROUP BEING ORGANIZED

People interested in participating in a Friends of the Library (FOL) group for Elbin Library are invited to an organizational meeting at 7:30 pm on Tuesday, October 24, in the Walnut Room of the student union.

For some time a number of people have felt the necessity of such a group on campus to focus attention on the needs of the library and to enlist support in addressing some of these needs. Last spring a committee began to lay the groundwork for FOL by drafting a constitution and bylaws for the organization.

Membership in the Friends of the Library is open to anyone. Annual dues have been established at several levels, including student ($1), regular ($2), and contributing ($10). For more information or to make a membership donation, contact Librarian Donald R. Strong or Mrs. Constance Hein at the library.

## LIBRARY ORIENTATION OFFERED

For faculty who wish their students to have an introduction to the library, the library staff are offering orientation sessions this fall. Jeanne Schramm and Frances Stewart have revised their slide program, which may be used in these sessions. Faculty should call 336-8035 to make arrangements.

# *Dacus Focus*

## Ida Jane Dacus Library
## Winthrop College

Format: folder

Size: 8 1/2 by 11"

Color: buff

Number of pages: 5 - 10

Frequency: 2 per year

Annual cost: $500 - 1,000

Number of copies: 500 - 1,000

Audience: faculty, staff, administration, friends, other libraries in South Carolina, North Carolina, and Georgia

Editorial responsibility: rotating editor; professional librarian

Desktop software: Word Perfect 5.0

# DACUS  FOCUS

## SERVICES AND RESOURCES OF THE WINTHROP COLLEGE LIBRARY

No. 23                                                                                     May 1989

# "CARDS TO SCREENS" ONLINE CATALOG PROJECT ON SCHEDULE AT DACUS LIBRARY

The culmination of almost 15 years of planning and preparation is drawing near as the Dacus Library faculty and staff prepare for the installation of the "online public access catalog" (OPAC) this June.

Winthrop joins USC, Clemson, the College of Charleston, and Francis Marion as well as hundreds of other college libraries throughout the country, by implementing a computer based replacement of the venerable card catalog.

Once the OPAC is operational in Fall 1989 or Spring 1990, library users will be able to search the library's collection of books by entering author, title, or subject at a computer terminal. But not only these traditional methods of searching will be available. In addition, "keyword" searching of titles will be possible, allowing the user to enter a word or words and retrieve all records for books whose titles contain those words. It will also be possible to limit results to books published during a certain time period, in a certain language, and in many other ways.

One of the handiest features of the upcoming catalog is the ability to determine which issues of a magazine the library owns. Instead of consulting the microfiche serials holdings list, a student can enter the name of the magazine on an OPAC terminal and find out if the latest issue has arrived, when the next issue is expected, what volumes are bound, etc.

The library began preparing for the online catalog in 1975, when we joined the Southeastern Library Network (SOLINET). Since that time, all cataloging of library materials has been computerized and records for books acquired before 1975 have been converted to machine readable form.

In 1981, Dacus Library installed a computerized circulation system to keep track of library materials checked out by patrons. In 1986, a system to provide ordering and tracking functions for books and periodicals was bought from Innovative Interfaces, Inc, of Berkeley, California. The OPAC system to be installed in June was also developed by Innovative and will interact with the ordering and periodicals system. Some other libraries using the Innovative system include the University of Maine, Wellesley College, the University of California at San Diego. the University of Oregon, and Oglethorpe College.

**Laurance R. Mitlin**
**Assistant Dean of Library Services**

# BUSY, BUSY, BUSY

It's the Tuesday after spring break and the students are everywhere. Tables and carrels on all three floors are filled with students quietly studying or working in groups. Many are huddled around the indexes or CD-ROM workstations and there's a ceaseless flurry of activity at the card catalog. The two reference librarians are busily answering a never-ending barrage of questions. Students are lined up at the circulation desk checking  out books, returning materials, using the reserve collection, or taking care of fines. Just another typical night in the Dacus Library.

Use of the library has increased dramatically over the past several years. Last year alone nearly a quarter million students and faculty visited the library. Circulation increased 8%, interlibrary loan 26%, reference questions 5%, and documents questions 54% (!) over the previous academic year. And this trend shows no signs of lessening: circulation, for example, is already up 6% over last year and interlibrary loan requests have increased a whopping 28%.

The nature of reference service is also changing. Whereas in the past most questions could be answered quickly, reference librarians are finding that it now takes much longer to help a student. This change is the result of an increased complexity in the questions asked combined with newer access tools (CD-ROM indexes, for example) that require more sophisticated research techniques. The process should become even lengthier with the advent of the online catalog.

The library is making scheduling and staffing adjustments in response to this increased demand for service. Because of heavy reference use at night, double coverage of the reference desk is now provided Monday through Wednesday evenings. Documents reference coverage was reduced to accommodate this change. For reference assistance in the documents area after 6:00 p.m. on weekdays, come to the main floor reference desk.

Students have also asked for reference coverage on Saturdays. Until now the library was unable to provide Saturday reference service. Recently permission was given to replace the interlibrary loan technical assistant position with a library faculty position. Because of this change, the library began Saturday reference coverage on April 1.

We are pleased that the students and faculty are making greater use of the library and its resources. Use is what we are about.

**Bob Gorman**
**Head of Pubic Services**

---

# NEW IN THE LIBRARY

From July 1, 1988, to March 15, 1989, the library added 5,074 new books to the collection. The average price per book was $24.08. This is below the *Publisher's Weekly* average price of $38.39. Orders were placed with over 75 different publishers or vendors. The most expensive purchase was the new edition of the *Oxford English Dictionary*.

New additions to the library also include subscriptions for 303 new serial titles. Payments for 88 of these titles have been made at an average cost of $72.17.

**Ginny Vesper**
**Head of Monographs Acquisitions Department**

**Gale Teaster-Woods**
**Head of Serials Department**

# PRESERVING THE FUTURE

In 1986 the Palmetto Archives, Libraries and Museums Council on Preservation (PALMCOP), in conjunction with the Southeastern Library Network (SOLINET), and with funding from the National Endowment for the Humanities (NEH), began a cooperative project of statewide needs assessment and preservation planning in South Carolina. This project is to serve as a model for other southeastern states.

This cooperative effort is necessary in South Carolina for several reasons. First, repositories in South Carolina hold a wealth of collections that are inadequately preserved; second, the librarians, curators, and archivists lack adequate preservation expertise; and third, insufficient funding of repositories makes it necessary to address these preserva- 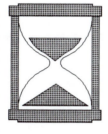 tion issues through a cooperative effort.

Winthrop became a member of PALMCOP at its inception. Gloria Kelley, Assistant Head of Technical Services, serves on its board of directors. When the project was funded by the National Endowment for the Humanities, the plan was to train a number of preservation specialists for the state. Seven individuals from various types of institutions were selected by the PALMCOP Board of Directors based upon their preservation expertise. They were trained to conduct preservation needs assessment visits. Ms. Kelley was selected from Winthrop along with six other people from various institutions in South Carolina.

The interns participated in an intensive training seminar June 13-17, 1988, at the Charleston Museum. The seminar was conducted by Lisa Fox, SOLINET Preservation Program Director, and Karen Matylewski of the Northeast Document Conservation Center. The seminar was needed to ensure that all interns had the same high level of competency on preservation matters, to develop a consistent preservation philosophy, and to provide guidance that would enable the interns to develop realistic recommendations to help the various institutions.

For six months, the interns visited public and private colleges, public records offices, county libraries, historical societies, and public libraries in South Carolina to access their preservation needs. Every institution visited received a written report of the findings and recommendations for preservation improvement.

Winthrop was one of the 24 institutions selected for a preservation site visit. On December 13, 1988, two interns and Lisa Fox visited Winthrop. The preliminary findings indicate that Dacus Library lacks adequate protection from water and fire, that the building has structural damage, that the collections lack protection from light damage, that more preservation staff is needed, and that the highly acidic microfilm boxes need to be replaced. Once the final report is received in April, the library will begin to concentrate on correcting some of the problems cited.

Finally, based on the information gathered during the institutional surveys, the interns will assess the state's preservation needs, problems, and resources. This information will  lead to the development of an action plan with recommendations for cooperative statewide preservation activities and suggestions for institutionalizing preservation responsibilities among existing state-level agencies and organizations.

Dacus Library is excited about the statewide effort and looks forward to working with various other institutions involved in the PALMCOP process.

**Gloria Kelley**
**Assistant Head of Technical Services**

# DEN OF ANTIQUITY

Since the last issue of *Dacus Focus* appeared, the following developments have occurred:

The Archives participated in the South Carolina Historical Records Assessment Project sponsored by the South Carolina Department of Archives and History and by the National Historical Publications Records Commission.

Gina Price conducted an oral history workshop at the Presbyterian Study Center in Montreat, North Carolina.

In August 1988, the space in Archives was reorganized to make more room for researchers and staff.

The Archives published "The Winthrop College Archives and Special Collections: A Guide to Its Manuscripts and Oral History Collections" in August 1988. The guide, which is being sold to the public for $15, is designed to create greater public awareness of the department's holdings.

In August the York Observer began publishing a series of photos from the Robert Ward Photograph Collection.

The Archives presented several showings of the rare 1919 Winthrop film and received some more films depicting Winthrop in the 1940's.

The Archivist visited Nicaragua in November 1988 and conducted research on Nicaraguan libraries. An article, the product of the research, appeared in the March 1989 issue of *American Libraries*, the largest circulating library publication in the U.S. The Archivist also gave several talks and slide-show presentations based on his trip to Nicaragua.

The Archives staff has been busy providing service for a variety of interesting patrons. Some of their research topics include: a pictorial history of York County; the history of Winthrop College; Black traditions in the Catawba region; attendance policy at Winthrop; women's higher education in the South; the home extension movement in South Carolina; South Carolina family history; Catawba Indians; oral history of South Carolina women; the history of the Rock Hill Junior Welfare League; and a biography of Grace Freeman.

**Ron Chepesiuk**
**Head of Archives and Special Collections**

# INTRODUCING THE DEBIT CARD

The library's public access photocopy service is about to undergo a radical change. In addition to buying four new photocopiers, the library will switch from a coin-operated system to a debit card system. This change became necessary because of the tremendous increase in the use of photocopiers. An inordinate amount of staff time is spent counting change, filling the change vending machine, and servicing the photocopiers. Under the new system patrons will purchase vend cards encoded with amounts of $1, $5, $10, or $20. The cards are used to activate the copiers. As copies are made, the cost is debited against the amount encoded on the card. Staff will no longer have to keep up with massive amounts of nickels, dimes, and quarters. The students should also find the system more convenient. They will not need change to make copies and vend cards can be retained and reencoded when more copying is necessary.

The library is also planning to add three public access microfilm/fiche copiers in the documents area. At present students fill out request slips to have photocopies of microfilm or microfiche made. Because these requests are growing by leaps and bounds (one day recently over 1,000 copies were made), students frequently are waiting 24 hours to get their copies. The new microfilm/fiche copiers will eliminate this problem. Since these copiers will be compatible with the debit card system, students will be able to make their own copies.

**Bob Gorman**
**Head of Pubic Services**

# CD-ROM COMES TO DACUS LIBRARY

It's time to begin researching for your term paper. You go to the reference desk and ask the reference librarian on duty where to find information on your topic. He or she suggests you look up your subject on one of the CD-ROM's. "Seedy Rom," you say to yourself. "What on earth is that?"

The term may sound strange to those who are unfamiliar with it, but CD-ROM is nothing more than a compact disk (CD) which has information "written" on it. Dacus Library currently subscribes to five CD-ROM products. Four of these are indexes to articles in journals and magazines: *ERIC*, the *Humanities Index*, the *Business Periodicals Index*, and the *Social Sciences Index*. The fifth product is *Disclosure*, a source of information on major U.S. corporations. Dacus Library also subscribes to the paper copy of all the CD-ROM products mentioned here except *Disclosure*. All four indexes are updated quarterly; *Disclosure* is updated monthly. And since all five systems provide menu screens from which options are chosen, even the novice user can learn to access information quickly.

*ERIC* (Educational Resources Information Center) indexes journals and other documents in the area of education and covers the years from 1980 to the present. You can obtain a printout of your ERIC search results in various formats, including a format which provides an abstract or summary of the article indexed. A guide sheet for use with ERIC is available at the reference desk.

The *Business Periodicals Index*, as its name implies, covers business-related articles from June 1982 to the present. The *Social Sciences Index* includes the years from April 1983 to the present. The

*Humanities Index* covers indexing from February 1984 to the present. These three indexes provide bibliographic citations only. A simple print function allows the user to develop a customized bibliography of search results.

The final CD-ROM product in Dacus Library, *Disclosure*, provides extensive company information for the last five years. In addition to obtaining a printout of search results, it is possible to download records from *Disclosure* to a spreadsheet or other program. (Consult a reference librarian for more information about this option.) A guide sheet for use with *Disclosure* is available at the reference desk.

One important point to note about the four CD-ROM indexes mentioned here is that Dacus Library does not have all the journals/magazines indexed. It is necessary to consult the serials holdings list to ascertain whether or not the library has the journal or magazine you need. If we do not carry a particular title, it may be possible to acquire an article for you through our interlibrary loan service. Inquire at the reference desk for further information about this service.

Dacus Library has plans for adding more CD-ROM products in the near future, including the *General Science Index* (the library currently subscribes to the paper copy) and *MARCIVE*, an index to U.S. government documents. In addition, the reference department is looking into the possibility of a CD-ROM network. A network would allow a patron to access any of the CD-ROM indexes form one workstation. As it is now, each workstation accesses only one index.

For further information about any of the CD--ROM products mentioned here, please ask at the reference desk. The reference librarian on duty will be happy to answer your questions or assist you in performing a search on one of the CD-ROM's.

**Miranda Halterlein**
**Online Search Librarian**

# ACTIVE PEOPLE

RON CHEPESIUK, Head of Archives and Special Collections, is serving on the Nominating Committee and the Directory Committee of the College and University Section of the Society of American Archivists. He is a member of the Archives Review Committee of the South Carolina Library Association.

ROSE-ELLEN ECKBERG, Documents Librarian, is Secretary of the Government Documents Roundtable of the South Carolina Library Association.

GERI GASKILL, Head of the Circulation Department, was recently recognized for 10 years of service to Winthrop College.

ROBERT (BOB) GORMAN, Head of Public Services, is Vice President/President-Elect of the Metrolina Library Association. He also serves as Chair of the Program Committee.

GLORIA KELLEY, assistant head of Technical Services, was selected as one of seven preservation interns in South Carolina. This internship is a pilot project sponsored by the Palmetto Archives, Libraries and Museums Council on Preservation (PALMCOP), the Southeastern Library Network (SOLINET), and the National Endowment for the Humanities (NEH).

CAROL MCIVER, Head of Technical Services, is a member of the Scholarship Committee of the North American Serials Interest Group (NASIG).

SANDY PAKOZDY, Monographs Acquisitions Department, was recently recognized for 10 years of service to Winthrop College.

SUSAN SILVERMAN, Head of the Reference Department, is serving on the Executive Board of the South Carolina Library Association as Chair of the Public Services Section. She is working with the section planning a fall workshop to include state public, academic, and school librarians. Also as a member of the Executive Board, she is involved with the program planning for the annual convention.

SHIRLEY TARLTON, Dean of Library Services, chaired the Charlotte Area Educational Consortium (CAEC) ad hoc committee that developed a library joint borrower's card for faculty members of CAEC institutions. She is also a member of an international bibliographic standards committee jointly sponsored by the American Library Association (ALA) and the International Federation of Library Associations (IFLA). This committee is developing an international machine-readable format for bibliographic information (MARBI). Dean Tarlton attended a recent meeting of the Association of College and Research Libraries' Women Academic Library Directors Network. She was instrumental in securing a Library Services and Construction Act (LSCA) grant to purchase fax machines for South Carolina libraries. Dean Tarlton also was recognized at a recent faculty meeting for her 20 years' service to Winthrop.

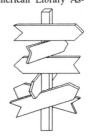

GALE TEASTER-WOODS, Head of the Serials Department, will chair the Committee on Student Development for the Southern Association of Colleges and Schools (SACS) reaccreditation visit.

VIRGINIA (GINNY) VESPER, Head of the Monographs Acquisitions Department, attended an American Library Association preconference in New Orleans on "Collection Development in the Electronic Age". She also attended an acquisitions conference at the College of Charleston.

Dacus Library would like to introduce the following replacement staff members:

**SANDRA DOUGLAS,** Library Technical Assistant in the Binding and Preservation Unit

**LOIS WALKER,** Reference Librarian and Coordinator of Interlibrary Loan

The following staff members are temporary employees of Dacus Library:

**JINILYN ANDERSON,** Library Technical Assistant IV in the Serials Department

**PARKY GETTYS,** Library Technical Assistant IV in the Serials Department

The following staff members have changed positions within Dacus Library:

**KAREN KOTERBA,** transferred from Library Technical Assistant III in the Binding and Preservation Unit to Library Technical Assistant IV in the Documents Department.

The following staff members had position upgrades in Dacus Library:

**DOROTHY (DOT) BARBER,** from Accounting Technician I to Library Technical Assistant IV

**BRENDA KNOX,** from Library Technical Assistant III in Circulation to Library Technical Assistant IV

**SANDY PAKOZDY,** from Library Technical Assistant III in Monographs Acquisitions to Library Technical Assistant IV

**ANN THOMAS,** from temporary Stack Supervisor in Circulation to permanent Stack Supervisor

The following staff members have resigned:

**DOROTHY BERRY,** Library Technical Assistant IV in the Interlibrary Loan Unit

**JOAN WATERS,** Clerical Specialist C in the Dean's Office

*Dacus Focus* is published twice a year by the staff of Dacus Library.

Comments and suggestions should be directed to the editor:

Robert M. Gorman, Dacus Library, Winthrop College, Rock Hill, SC 29733

**Dacus Library**
**Winthrop College**
**Rock Hill, SC 29733**

# Library Produced Newsletters

# A: *newsletter*

## Millsaps - Wilson Library
## Millsaps College

Format: folder

Size: 8 1/2 by 14"

Color: varies

Number of pages: 1 - 4

Frequency: bi-monthly

Annual cost: $0 - 500

Number of copies: 150 - 300

Audience: faculty, staff, administration, and students

Editorial responsibility: permanent editor; professional librarian

Desktop software: Word Perfect

MILLSAPS COLLEGE

Volume 2, No. 2
November, 1989

Information from
the Millsaps-Wilson Library

A: newsletter
A: newsletter
A: newsletter
A: newsletter
A: newsletter
A: newsletter

MILLSAPS - WILSON LIBRARY, MILLSAPS COLLEGE

### KD's Celebrate 75th With Gift to Library

The Mu chapter of the Kappa Delta sorority celebrated the 75th anniversary of its founding with activities on November 11 that included donating to the Millsaps-Wilson Library the 1989, second edition of the Oxford English Dictionary. A reception for sorority members, faculty and others featured a brief ceremony. College Librarian Jim Parks accepted the generous gift on behalf of the students and faculty of the College. The OED, called "the greatest work in dictionary making ever undertaken" by the New York Times when it was first published in 1933 after 75 years of preparation, has been enlarged to include changes in the English language over the past 50 years. It now includes almost 500,000 entries illustrated by over 2,000,000 quotations. A monument to the history and development of the English language, the 20 volume OED will replace the first edition and its supplements. The library is especially grateful to the KD's for their generous support in providing an essential reference resource to the campus. The dictionary will eventually sit in a custom-made stand with a plaque honoring the Kappa Delta sorority.

Jim Parks
College Librarian

### New Acquisitions

One Village in China, a three-part video series, was purchased with the Ford grant to support a new course on life in China being developed by Dr. Yoko Baba. The three tapes are entitled "All Under Heaven; Life in a Chinese Village," "Small Happiness; Women of a Chinese Village," "To Taste a Hundred Herbs; Gods, Ancestors and Medicine in a Chinese Village."

**Copyright notice recently encountered:** All material contained herein is copyright 1985, 1988 by Human Synergistics, Inc. We would be most displeased if anyone should reproduce any part of it without our express permission. While we're not vengeful, we are provokable.

### Interact with the Catalog

The library's CD-ROM catalog has many features that are often overlooked. Two of these are LOCAL INFO and MAKE NOTES. Press the Local Info key for Library news and reminders, or campus news, if submitted to the librarian. To save notes to yourself or for the library staff, press the Make Notes key. Notes on your searches can be reclaimed later or you can leave suggestions. Notes are checked frequently; announcements are changed weekly. Try these and other functions of the catalog to get the most out of it.

### New Books Area
New books are now kept on shelves in the Catalog Alcove. Book jackets of notable new books are also on display.

## Library Hours Compared

One of the most popular topics for discussion about libraries is their hours of service. The staff periodically surveys other libraries to see how we compare. The most recent informal survey was of universities in Mississippi. What follows is a condensed version of their schedules. While there are many cautions which apply, the most important one is to acknowledge the distinction between small, private liberal arts colleges and state-supported universities with large enrollments and many graduate programs.

### Millsaps College
(5 librarians, 5 staff)

| | |
|---|---|
| Mon-Thur | 8 a.m. - 12 a.m. |
| Fri | 8 a.m. - 5 p.m. |
| Sat | 9 a.m. - 5 p.m. |
| Sun | 2 p.m. - 12 a.m. |

### Mississippi State University
(23 librarians, 29 staff)

| | |
|---|---|
| Mon-Thur | 7:45 a.m. - 12 a.m. |
| Fri | 7:45 a.m. - 5 p.m. |
| Sat | 9:00 a.m. - 6 p.m. |
| Sun | 2:00 p.m. - 12 a.m. |

### Jackson State University
(10 librarians, 19 staff)

| | |
|---|---|
| Mon-Thur | 7:50 a.m. - 11 p.m. |
| Fri | 7:50 a.m. - 6 p.m. |
| Sat | 8:00 a.m. - 4 p.m. |
| Sun | 4:00 p.m. - 10 p.m. |

### University of Mississippi
(21 librarians, 29 staff)

| | |
|---|---|
| Mon-Thur | 8 a.m. - 11 p.m.  * |
| Fri | 8 a.m. - 10 p.m. |
| Sat | 10 a.m. - 6 p.m. |
| Sun | 1 p.m. - 11 p.m. |

* study area open til 1 a.m.

### Mississippi College
(10 librarians, 5 staff)

| | |
|---|---|
| Mon-Thur | 7:45 a.m. - 10 p.m. |
| Fri | 7:45 a.m. - 5 p.m. |
| Sat | 9:00 a.m. - 4 p.m. |
| Sun | 2:00 p.m. - 5 p.m. |

### Univ. of Southern Mississippi
(18 librarians, 20 staff)

| | |
|---|---|
| Mon-Thur | 7:30 a.m. - 11 p.m. |
| Fri | 7:30 a.m. - 8 p.m. |
| Sat | 9:00 a.m. - 5 p.m. |
| Sun | 1:00 a.m. - 11 p.m. |

### U. S. Documents

A computer program, PFS: Professional File, is now being used to keep government document records. The program enables the staff to process new items in less than half the time previously needed. Special thanks to student Monica Meeks for setting up this helpful system.

Check the U. S. Documents Subject Bibliographies for lists of publications available from the Government Printing Office. The titles, ranging from Accounting to X-Rays, reflect the wide range of government printing. See Mrs. Lewis.

### New on InfoTrac CD-ROM Index

A new feature has been added to the Academic Index. A user can now see on the screen which entries are in periodicals owned by Millsaps. The Academic Index covers over 400 titles; the Millsaps library carries over half.

The public service staff is conducting an informal survey of users of the CD-ROM indexes. We'll appreciate your help in filling out one of the brief forms kept at the CD-ROM workstations.

### How to Use the Library

Handouts offering help in using library resources are kept at the Main Desk. Some examples are: "How to Find Information on a Corporation," "How to Use Moody's Manuals," and "Finding Articles in Periodicals." Help us help you. Suggestions for topics for information handouts are always welcome. See Mrs. Harmon.

### Successful Book Sale

Homecoming was a colorful and happy occasion. For its part, the library sponsored a booksale of duplicate gifts and made over $400 for the book fund. Book shoppers carried away hardbacks for $1 and paperbacks for 25 cents. The staff all participated, dressed in purple library shirts for the occasion. Thanks to all who came by.

**A: newsletter, p. 3**

**From the Archives**

Founders Hall Lives!

An interesting request came to the Archives recently when Joyce Crotchett of Brandon called to ask about the history of Founders Hall. Her home, which is to be on the Lions Club Christmas tour, was built with the brick from Founders which was razed in 1973, and she needed information for a brochure.

Founders stood from 1885 to 1973 just about where the proposed new library will be. In 1883 the Natchez Seminary (Baptist) moved to this North State Street site and changed its name to Jackson College. The president lived in the plantation home known later as Elsinore and classes met at Mt. Helms Baptist Church until construction was complete on a $12,500, three story brick building. Male students were hired to help with the construction, which may explain the initials and other writing on some of the bricks. The upper two floors became dormitory rooms, classes met on the first floor and the assembly hall was in the basement. Five years after its completion Millsaps College was built facing North West Street, but adjacent to Jackson College. In 1901 an offer from Major Millsaps to buy the property for $40,000 was accepted and in 1902 Jackson College moved to temporary quarters across town.

Millsaps used Founders Hall first as a dormitory and in 1911 it became the Millsaps Preparatory School. In January, 1913, fire destroyed much of the structure. It was rebuilt, altering the appearance somewhat. Later Founders became a women's dorm and, still later, offices.

Gerry Reiff
College Archivist

---

**EXAM/HOLIDAY HOURS**

Thanksgiving
The library will close at 5:00 p.m. on Wednesday, November 22 and reopen at 8:00 a.m. on Monday, November 27.

Exam Week
Library hours on Friday, December 15, will be extended to Midnight.

Christmas
The library will close at 5:00 p.m. on Thursday, December 21 and reopen Monday, January 8.

Between Semesters
The library will be open for limited service 8:30 - 4:30, Monday - Friday, January 8 to January 16. Full schedule resumes Wednesday, January 17.

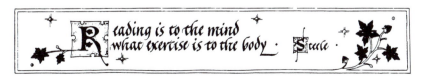
Reading is to the mind what exercise is to the body · Steele ·

# What's happening at Oesterle Library

## Oesterle Library
## North Central College

Format: folder

Size: 8 1/2 by 11"

Color: white

Number of pages: 1 - 4

Frequency: 3 per year

Annual cost: $0 - 500

Number of copies: 150 - 300

Audience: faculty, staff, and administration

Editorial responsibility: permanent editor; professional librarian

Desktop software: no

OESTERLE LIBRARY, NORTH CENTRAL COLLEGE

WHAT'S HAPPENING AT

OESTERLE LIBRARY

FALL TERM

1989

library has implemented as part of its LCS system. Barb also spent a great deal of time implementing the new OCLC CAT-CD 450 system, acquired by the library during the summer. This system involves two new Wyse Computer terminals and several compact disk players which are used by staff to search the cataloging database offline in off hours, then download records to floppy disks where they can be massaged into NCC records, and finally batch sent via modem and phone lines to OCLC in Ohio.

****************

## THE GREAT LIBRARY BOOKSALE

The accumulation of gift books over the course of the past year was dealt with by means of a "massive" book sale from October 19 to October 25. The library sold most of several thousand volumes and made well over $500 which will be entirely devoted to purchasing additional overhead projectors. Book loving faculty members found a number of "gems." One found a first edition of a little-known Stephen Crane novel worth almost $100 in the book trade.

****************

## SOME NEW LIBRARY EQUIPMENT

Over the summer and fall the library has acquired some new equipment which we believe will do much to support in-class instruction and more efficient library use. Beginning in Winter Term, the library will have a portable projection TV and videocassette player which can be checked out and used in classrooms. Essentially, this projection TV provides the same kind and quality of image as does the TV in A.V. room 10. We will begin booking reservations for this equipment over interim.

The library also acquired four compact disk players, three of which are portable and may be checked out of the library by students, faculty and staff. Although the library has a very modest CD collection, in the debate over chickens or eggs, we opted to get the chicken first. We are formulating policies on the use of the CD players now, and they should be ready by January.

The library finally had the funds to purchase a new microfilm reader/printer, thus replacing a 15 year old machine which used very expensive light-sensitive paper. With

the purchase of one more machine in the near future, the library will have sufficient photocopiers for its extensive fiche and film collections.

The library combined resources with the Maintenance Department to supply permanent screens to 11 classrooms in the Fall Term. Our long-term goal is to make sure all classrooms have both screens and overhead projectors.

*****************

## ACQUISITIONS

The library has acquired a number of important reference books you might be interested in knowing about. One of the most important is International Marketing Data & Statistics (1988/89). Anyone who has tried to find relatively recent demographic, consumer, or economic information about other countries knows what a challenge it can be. This work is the best single source for providing that sort of recent information. Along the same lines, the library has purchased the very important Standard Directory of Advertisers (1989) and Standard Directory of Advertising Agencies. Also in business and marketing, you should be aware that we now have Metro Insights, an analysis of 100 U.S. metro markets, Employment and Earnings, a government source for current employment and salary information, Moody's International Manual, and Best's Insurance Reports.

You can deduce from some of these titles, that we are attempting to upgrade the reference collection for international business. This is a subject field where current information is hard (and expensive) to come by, but we feel it is important enough to devote considerable resources for curricular support.

Other interesting recent acquisitions in the Reference collection include Virginia McAlester's A Field Guide to American Houses, Oxford Textbook of Medicine (the first medical textbook we've purchased in many years), Television and Ethics: A Bibliography, and a new encyclopedia for a very important subject field, Encyclopedia of Information Systems and Services produced by Gale Research Corporation.

## WHAT'S HAPPENING AT OESTERLE LIBRARY

The library produces this newsletter each term to keep faculty and staff informed of services, acquisitions, and other changes which might be important to the NCC community. The lateness with which the newsletter comes out this time is an indication of how hectic this term has been for the library.

## 1988/89 ACADEMIC YEAR STATISTICS

The library is monitoring three crucial areas of library usage. Statistics for the last academic year---as well as preliminary statistics for the Fall Term this year--- indicate substantial increases in periodical interlibrary loans, LCS interlibrary borrowing, and A.V. equipment usage, particularly overhead projectors.

Total interlibrary loans went up 23% last year, rising from 6,982 items borrowed and loaned in 1987/88 to 8,601 in 1988/89. When you consider that the library did 1,790 total interlibrary loan transactions in 1985, a 30% increase in five years indicates a brisk business indeed. We still borrow more than we loan, but the gap is closing. As an example, in 1987/88 we borrowed just about twice as many photocopied articles as we loaned. Last year, however we received 946 articles and sent 889.

LCS interlibrary book borrowing continued to rise by very healthy numbers. We borrowed nearly 1,000 more books last year than the year before, and loaned over 300 more. Our overall use of other libraries increased by a very robust 28%.

Interlibrary loaning has become more than just another service offered to students, faculty and staff; it has become a necessity in the support of the curriculum. It is labor intensive, however, so a large increase of the magnitude of 25% is a cause for concern. Between academic 1987/88 and 1988/89 the increase in photocopies sent out required about 6.5 extra work hours per week for the 30 weeks of term.

The third service area to increase tremendously is the use of A.V. equipment, particularly overhead projectors and 1/2" video players. Term assignments for overheads went from 49 in academic 1987/88 to 59 classes in 1988/89, while individual class use went from 532 in 87/88 to 606 in 1988/89. There were, literally, many times when faculty asked for overheads and there were none available. Preliminary use statistics for the Fall Term 1989 indicate that demand went up still higher. The library has purchased half a dozen additional overheads and a new VCR/TV to attempt to keep up with this crucial area of curricular support.

We feel one cause for the increase in library use is our bibliographic instruction program. We did 73 bibliographic instruction sessions last year with 1273 student contact hours. We have already done 36 bibliographic instructions in the Fall Term 1989 with 663 student contact hours. We believe that educative function drives library use, and faculty involvement in the bibliographic instruction sessions enhances that library education. As a point of comparison in academic 1984/85 there were 9 bibliographic instructions and 210 student contact hours.

******************

## STAFF ACTIVITIES IN THE FALL TERM 1989

Many of you are probably aware of the key changes in the library this term. Kelly Collins joined the staff as a Public Services Librarian in July. A graduate of Knox College, she has an M.A. in History from Northern Illinois University, and will be receiving an M.L.S. from the same university in December. She has been given responsibility for interlibrary loan as well as reference and bibliographic instruction duties.

Both Kelly and Alan Willis now have offices on the second floor in the old archives room. The archives are now in an area right behind the staff work room on the first floor.

Belinda Cheek has been relieved of interlibrary loan responsibilities and has begun cataloging a large backlog of gift books. Belinda anticipates receiving her M.L.S. degree from Northern in June 1990. She will become the sixth professional librarian on staff.

Belinda and Sally Chipman organized the first ever student assistant training day on Saturday, September 16. The library was given leave to close for nearly the entire day to provide a rational and coherent training session for all returning and new student assistants. The entire library staff participated in what was a very successful training program. In the past training was spread over many days with a great deal of redundancy and wasted effort as a result. The staff hopes this annual training day can be built permanently into the academic year cycle.

In other staff news, Ed Meachen was elected Chair of the Illinois Library Computer Systems Organization (ILCSO) Policy Council and President of ILCSO for an unprecedented third straight year. Over the past 18 months, the organization has accepted membership for six additional academic libraries, four of which are now online: the Illinois Mathematics & Science Academy, Roosevelt University, the School of the Art Institute, and Oakton Community College. National College of Education and Barat College have more recently been accorded membership.

Ed delivered a paper at the Illinois Association of College & Research Libraries Conference in DeKalb on November 2. It was entitled "The Book, the Machine, and the Library," and involved the fiscal, personnel, and psychological costs of networking for the small college library. He also attended a two day legislative workshop in Springfield in October. The workshop initiated a group of librarians involved with the Illinois Library Association Public Policy Committee into the vagaries of political lobbying.

Ed Meachen and Sally Chipman attended the annual Allerton Conference in late October sponsored by the University of Illinois Graduate Library School. Librarians from around the country discussed the issue of "Ethics and the Librarian," a particularly interesting issue from two perspectives: the FBI's new library awareness program, an attempt to coerce librarians into giving information about people who use library resources, and the perspective of North Central College's own Leadership, Ethics, and Values program. Ed and Sally will propose a faculty colloquium on the issue of library ethics for the Spring Term.

Sally Chipman also became chair of the Illinois OCLC User Education Committee, the group mostly responsible for training Illinois librarians in the use of the national cataloging database. On campus, Sally was one of the co-organizers of "Book Works," the very successful library exhibition of works by North Central College faculty and staff.

Barb Kosinsky and Mary Jo Clingman attended several days of workshops for the FAXON serials control system which the

# *Library News*

**Transylvania University Library**
**Transylvania University**

Format: stapled

Size: 8 1/2 by 11"

Color: white

Number of pages: 1 - 4

Frequency: 1 per semester

Annual cost: not known

Number of copies: 150 -300

Audience: faculty, staff, administration, and students

Editorial responsibility: permanent editor; public services librarian

Desktop software: MacWrite

# *** LIBRARY NEWS ***

Transylvania University           Issue 1  September 1989

## ACADEMIC INDEX

*Infotrac's* **ACADEMIC INDEX** is now available for the students, faculty and staff of Transylvania University. **ACADEMIC INDEX** is designed for research in a broad variety of subjects including Humanities, Social Sciences, General Science, and Current Events. The database, updated and cumulated monthly, allows users to search four years of periodicals and the most recent six months of the *New York Times*.

The new reference system is an index to over 390 scholarly and general interest periodicals, and the *New York Times*. The database is stored on CD-ROM and hundreds of thousands of periodical citations may be accessed through the computer. The system is fast and easy to use. A printed bibliography of relevant citations is available for each user. Instructions for use of the **ACADEMIC INDEX**, if requested, will be given on an individual basis.

* * * * *

## OXFORD ENGLISH DICTIONARY, 2nd edition

The library is pleased to announce the acquisition of the second edition of the **Oxford English Dictionary**. The **OED** Second Edition contains 59,000,000 words in its 290,500 main entries, and covers 616,500 word-forms. It boasts 2,412,400 illustrative quotations and 57,000 cross references. The new edition has 15 percent more main entries and 34 percent more volume than the First Edition.

This remarkable reference includes complete sense history, variant forms, pronunciation, etymology, and dated quotations illustrating the use of each word in context (with source given). Coverage extends over the whole of the general language, plus scientific and technical terms, slang, dialectical variations, and new vocabulary.

The *New York Times* calls this massive effort "the greatest work in dictionary making ever undertaken." The limited first print run has allocated only four thousand copies to the United States. Oxford University Press sees the Second Edition carrying well into the twenty-first century before a third edition will likely appear.

The **OED** is shelved in the library's Reference Room along with the First Edition.

## THE STACKS

The library's stacks have a slightly different look this year. The Library of Congress collection is now very generously spaced and the Dewey collection very compactly shelved on the third floor. The shifting was done in preparation for completing the reclassification of the Dewey collection, now in progress. This will make way for the merging of the two collections.

The new arrangement of the stacks is as follows:

Stacks A houses LC call numbers A-L
Stacks B houses LC call numbers M-Z
and Dewey call numbers 001-150
Stacks C houses Dewey call numbers 160-999
and the Dewey fiction section

* * * * *

## LIBRARY SERVICES CONTINUED IN 1989-90

The following library public services are available to all faculty (items #1 and 2 are also available to students):

**1. DIALOG** Information Services, Inc. is a collection of more than 300 databases representing every major field of study. From these databases bibliographic references to published literature, statistical tables, and business and financial data can be drawn. The online search will be scheduled 1-2 days after the completion of the search request form (available at the information desk). There is a $5.00 charge per search.

**2. INTERLIBRARY LOAN** services make it possible to extend the resources of the library by borrowing books and/or periodical articles from other institutions. Materials are usually received 1-2 weeks after the completion of the request form (available at the circulation desk). There is no charge for this service.

**3. JOURNAL HOTLINE** is a service offered to faculty members interested in the current contents of journals is their areas of study or interest. Any faculty member may request the Table of Contents of up to five journals subscribed to by Transylvania University Library.

**4. LIBRARY INSTRUCTION** may be requested for any interested classes. The instruction can be general library usage, or subject specific.

**5. BIBLIOGRAPHIES** of the library's holdings on any subject will be developed by the library staff per any faculty member's request.

**For information or questions concerning library services, contact Carolyn Tassie, 8225.**

# *Library Footnotes*

## Krannert Memorial Library
## University of Indianapolis
## Indianapolis, Indiana

Format: stapled

Size: 8 1/2 by 11"

Color: white

Number of pages: 1 - 4

Frequency: occasional

Annual cost: $0 -500

Number of copies: 0 - 150

Audience: faculty, staff, and administration

Editorial responsibility: permanent editor; library director

Desktop software: Newsmaster

# LIBRARY FOOTNOTES

*An Occasional Newsletter* **September, 1989**

## "Hello" to One and All !

The library staff says "hi" to new faculty and "welcome back" to returning friends. We hope your summer was great! As we launch into the fall semester, we thought a newsletter about the library would help remind you about our procedures and update you on a few changes. As the school year progresses, let us be of service in any way we can!

## Reserves

Library books, personal books or articles, boxes of bones, Indian baskets and projectile points—the library can put almost anything on Reserve for your students. You can select a check-out period of two hours, three days, or seven days, depending on the usage you expect. Bring the items for Reserve to the library (at the beginning of the semester, if possible) and fill out a Reserve slip indicating the period selected, the title of the item and the semesters for which you

want it kept on Reserve. We provide a computer printout of Reserve items sorted by professor. Please note the importance of identifying your Reserve item to us for the printout in the same terms that you use on your syllabus and in class so that students can find it easily. It is imperative that you bring your Reserve items to the library at least two days before assigning them to students so that we can process them and get them on the computer printout.

## Who Orders the Books?

Primary responsibility for ordering library materials (books, periodicals, audio-visuals) rests with the faculty. The library's collection development staff assist by filling in gaps, ordering in cross-disciplinary fields, and maintaining the Reference collection. To order books, faculty send requests to departmental chairpersons or school deans for approval, and these requests come to the library for ordering. Each department and school has a purchase allocation for the year. On March 1st, any unspent monies revert to the library's general fund

which we use to place orders over an allocation or for general improvements. The library has a Collection Development Policy, adopted by the faculty, which provides selection guidelines; it is on permanent Reserve for easy access. When new books have been received and processed and are available to be checked out, the faculty member who ordered them is notified.

## Library Book Check Out

Faculty may check out books for the academic year by showing their ID card; the due date is the following August 1st. Faculty may check out audio-visual items for one week. Periodicals and Reference books do not circulate, but special arrangements can be made to take one to class.

# Ordering Journals

Purchasing new journals for the library involves a long term commitment of funds. Requests for new subscriptions are channeled through chairpersons/ deans to the Library Committee which reviews them twice annually (November and March). Approved requests are forwarded to the Library Director and will be purchased if funds are available. As with books, the library's primary mission to support the curriculum and only secondarily to support faculty research should be taken into consideration in all requests.

# Conference Rooms

Did you know that the library has two conference rooms which can be scheduled for meetings or classes? Unfortunately, neither room is very large, but they can be handy if a location in the library would be appropriate for a meeting.

# Library Classes

The Reference Librarian offers classes in library use

to any faculty members who would like to integrate what librarians call "bibliographic instruction" into their classes. These sessions can be general ones introducing the library and how information is organized or in-depth classes on doing research in a particular discipline. Classes should be scheduled with the Reference Librarian.

# Microforms

The library's collections include microfilm and microfiche materials, primarily retrospective issues of magazines, journals, and newspapers. Equipment for using microforms includes readers and printers for each format. These formats save space and eliminate vandalism of hard copy materials.

# Computer Searches

Need help with your research? The library offers free computer searches to faculty. Using the DIALOG system, we have access to hundreds of computer databases which can be searched for citations to information on your topic of

interest. Due to the high cost of online access, a preliminary interview with the Reference Librarian is required.

# Interlibrary Loan

This library does not have every item you may need—but we will surely try to get it for you! Using our computer network OCLC, we can locate materials in other libraries and can request to borrow or photocopy them. Thus, we can extend our library beyond the local walls and access libraries elsewhere.

# Faculty Photocopying

The library has two photocopy machines and will be adding a third very soon. Faculty members may make copies at the library and charge them to their department or school subject, of course, to chairperson/dean policies. At the library, the faculty member shows his/her I.D. card and requests the copier bypass key at the Circulation Desk. First time users will be shown where it is inserted in the machine. A count of copies made should be kept so that when the key is returned the copier notebook can be signed and the number of copies noted.

# ZOOM--Fax Arrives

Telefacsimile has come to the library! We have purchased a "fax" machine which will be used primarily for interlibrary loan of short articles, as well as for asking and answering reference questions. The machine is available to send and receive faculty and administrative items as well. Long distance calls will be billed to departments or schools. Library staff will operate the equipment and will telephone any recipient of a "faxed" item for pick up.

# What Do We Own?

Everybody knows that the card catalog is, essentially, a multi-access list of books that the library owns. Periodicals, however, are not cataloged and, thus, do not appear in the card catalog. The library maintains a computer database of periodicals holdings and provides a printout of titles and where they are located in the building. These printouts are located in many places around the library. Because the

periodical database includes departmental/subject codes, lists of titles sorted by department/school can be provided upon request. The library's audio-visual holdings (records, compact disks, filmstrips, videotapes, and audio-cassettes) are cataloged like books and, thus, are accessible through the card catalog. However, a computer printout of all formats other than records is kept in the A-V Room and at the Circulation Desk for easy access by non-book format, if desired.

# Rare Books

The Fouts Rare Books Room houses a collection of various kinds of rare and unusual books. Its strengths lie in fine bindings and limited editions, although early printed books, first editions, signed works, and other types of rare books are represented. The collection also includes some examples of medieval manuscripts. Rare books may not be checked out but they are available for study or show to students by arrangement with the Library Director.

# The University Archives

The University Archives is located on the second floor of the library and is open several afternoons a week or anytime by appointment. The Archives houses the historical collections of papers, artifacts, and memorabilia of the university. In addition, it plays a museum function by storing and displaying materials of historical

interest donated by members of the university community but not specifically related to the school itself. The Archives also is the location of the library's EUB and Methodist book collections, as well as the collection of university yearbook, honors papers, and masters theses. Faculty members are encouraged not only to use the Archives for teaching and research but also to consider it as a place to house important papers and artifacts.

# Library Hours

Mon. - Thurs.
8:00 a.m. - 10:30 p.m.

Friday
8:00 a.m. - 7:00 p.m.

Saturday
9:00 a.m. - 5:00 p.m.

Sunday
1:00 p.m. - 10:30 p.m.

### LIBRARY STAFF
*Philip Young, Director*
*Shirley Bigna,*
*Assistant Director*
*Christine Guyonneau,*
*Reference Librarian*
*Linda Shaw,*
*Cataloging Librarian*
*Joy Caskey,*
*Circulation Supervisor*
*Susan Barhan,*
*Circulation Supervisor*
*Frances Graham,*
*Cataloging Assistant*
*Barbra Demaree,*
*Serials Assistant*
*Pam Olston,*
*Acquisitions Assistant*
*Lynn Berry,*
*Secretary/Archives*

# Commercially Produced Newsletters

# *Library Newsletter*

## James P. Magill Library
## Haverford College

Format:  folder

Size:  8 1/2 by 11"

Color:  buff

Number of pages:  1 - 4

Frequency:  2 per year

Annual cost:  $500 - 1,000

Number of copies:  500 - 1,000

Audience:  faculty, staff, administration, friends, other college libraries, and library retirees

Editorial responsibility:  rotating editor; professional librarian

Desktop software:  no

# LIBRARY

N E W S L E T T E R

October 1989    **HAVERFORD COLLEGE**    No. 6

## PHOTOGRAPHS AT HAVERFORD COLLEGE

What do Lehigh University, Princeton University, and Haverford College have in common? They are the only academic institutions in the tri-state area with photographic collections illustrating artistic practice in photography. How do these three institutions differ? Haverford is the only one with a tenured professor teaching the art of photography.

William E. Williams is that professor, and since 1979 he has helped the College acquire approximately 2700 images representing the work of 120 photographers. This collection, housed among the special collections of Magill Library, spans the history of the medium from its origins to the present. Thus, there are daguerreotypes, ferrotypes, and platinum prints as well as silver, gelatin, and bromide prints, type-C prints, and others. The artists represented in this collection read like a who's who in photography: Berenice Abbott, Ansel Adams, Diane Arbus, Eugène Atget, John Griscom Bullock, Julia Margaret Cameron, Harold Edgerton, Walker Evans, Lewis Hine, André Kertesz, Jacques-Henri Lartigue, Lisette Model, W. Eugene Smith, Jessie Wilcox Smith, Alfred Stieglitz, and James Van Der Zee. In the past year alone, photographs by Bernard Stehle, Doris Ulmann, Henri Cartier-Bresson, Arnold Genthe, William Henry Jackson, O. Winston Link, George Platt Lynes, William Rau, Todd Webb, and others have been added to the collection.

In 1902, John Griscom Bullock (Haverford, 1874), a widely exhibited proponent of photography as an art, joined Alfred Stieglitz to form a new society that would further the artistic recognition of pictorial photography; they called the society the Photo-Secession to indicate its independence from the academic art establishment. It is especially appropriate and fortunate that the Haverford collection has more than 70 Bullock prints in its collection, one-third of which were hung in a recent exhibition in Comfort Gallery.

1989 marks the sesquicentennial of Louis Daguerre's production of an image from life onto a chemically-treated-metal plate. Haverford College joins the many institutions, national and international, celebrating this anniversary by mounting two exhibits: one in the Sharpless Gallery of Magill Library from October through January, 1990; the other, "Photographs from the Permanent Collection," in the Comfort Gallery from March 31–May 6, 1990. Professor Williams will mount an exhibition of his own work in the Comfort Gallery from October 21–November 12, 1989.

—Diana Franzusoff Peterson

## BORGSTEDT CARTOONS GIVEN TO LIBRARY

Douglas Borgstedt '33 has given Magill Library over 250 cartoons he created as a syndicated cartoonist in the 1960's and 1970's. His work regularly appeared in over ninety newspapers around the country; from 1968 until it folded a decade later, Borgstedt gathered a national reputation as editorial cartoonist for the *Philadelphia Bulletin*.

The cartoons are some of the best examples of pictorial journalism to be found anywhere. His work covers a wide variety of political and social topics, and he managed to poke fun at nearly every important political figure active during two turbulent decades. Borgstedt's work combines sharp wit and savvy understanding of news events with an extraordinary artistic sense.

Borgstedt began producing cartoons while in college, contributing caricatures of some of his professors to the *Haverfordian*. Forced to drop out of college for financial reasons after his sophomore year, he began free-lancing and eventually began selling cartoons to the *Saturday Evening Post, Colliers,* and other magazines. In 1943, he became art editor of *Yank,* the Army weekly published for the troops fighting in the southwest Pacific and Far East. After the war, he returned to the *Saturday Evening Post* as photography editor and remained with the magazine until it closed in 1963. It was then that he began a full-time career as editorial cartoonist.

Today, his cartoons appear in a number of different business publications, and he is currently a weekly contributor to *Editor and Publisher* on the subject of press and television. He has even done work for the

# LIBRARY NEWSLETTER

National Football League. Winner of a number of Freedom Foundation awards, he has spoken on editorial cartooning at Ohio University, Washington and Lee University, and here at Haverford. Douglas Borgstedt resides with his wife in Valley Forge.

—Michael Freeman

## LIBRARY PUBLICATIONS

Scripture urges us not to put our light under a bushel but on a candlestick that all may see. Magill Library, too, does not want to keep its good works a secret and has several series of publications to enlighten users about services, collections, and subject areas that the Library's collections and services may be better known and easier to use.

Together with Canaday Library at Bryn Mawr College, we produce a set of eleven reference sheets describing library services, including online searching and interlibrary loan, branch libraries for music and the sciences, and special collections ranging from the Colleges' archives to documents published by the Organization for Economic Cooperation and Development. Because the Philadelphia region has such a wealth of academic and special research libraries, we also publish a reference sheet giving area libraries' addresses and hours as well as their access policies for Bryn Mawr and Haverford students and faculty.

In many courses at Haverford, students must do original research, for example, transcribing, editing, and analyzing an historic manuscript document for the seminar on historical evidence or researching a woman whose achievements deserve to be better known for a course on women in pre-industrial Europe. This work requires a sophisticated understanding of the research process and knowledge of a broad range of reference sources. To help students in their work, the Library, together with Bryn Mawr, has begun a series of research guides. The first title in the series is an eight-page introduction to library research; the other seven cover subject encyclopedias, book reviews, biographical information, subject bibliographies, primary sources, and off-campus sources. We have not yet finished the last three but expect to have them available before the end of the first semester.

In certain subject areas and for certain kinds of reference tools, publishing is voluminous, and the body of literature available requires a great deal of explanation, much more than can be accommodated in the four and eight-page reference guide series. To cover these larger topics, Haverford and Bryn Mawr have put together a number of reference booklets. The newest in the series is an 85-page guide to resources on women's studies. Over the last twenty years, the examination of women's roles has prompted major reevaluations of the traditions of scholarship; research

on women has been in the forefront of those studies that are reshaping both contemporary education and the structures of knowledge represented by the traditional academic disciplines. Publishing, both scholarly and popular, in women's studies has increased dramatically, and the Haverford/Bryn Mawr Booklet lists and describes the reference tools that give access to this literature. Microfilm sets, rare books and manuscripts, and faculty and staff with research interests in women's studies along with such familiar sources as bibliographies, encyclopedias, and periodical indexes are covered in the booklet.

Whenever reference librarians at Haverford talk to classes about research for a term paper or project, they compile specialized bibliographies and guides together with handouts that illustrate the use of specific reference tools, e.g., *Psyclit* or *Social Science Citation Index*. For a senior thesis group, a bibliography must cover the reference tools for an entire field, say, philosophy or religion; but since most courses are designed around a topic, most of the bibliographies we produce are similarly focused, e.g., "Sources for African and Latin American Labor History," "Selected Sources on the Society of Friends in China and Japan," and "Romantik," sources for research in German romanticism. During the course of one academic year, reference librarians prepare over forty such bibliographies for individual classes.

These guides and bibliographies serve the students' immediate needs for a particular class assignment. They also help in the long term, however, by showing the range of materials available, thereby suggesting either other topics for investigation or hitherto unrecognized approaches to or aspects of one with which a student may already be familiar. By identifying and describing specific sources not only at Haverford but also at Bryn Mawr, Swarthmore, the University of Pennsylvania, and beyond, the bibliographies both open up the information resources of the wider scholarly world and reveal the underlying organization of a discipline's literature. Samples of all the publications discussed above are available in the lobby of Magill.

—Margaret Schaus

## SOVIET LIBRARIAN VISITS MUSIC LIBRARY

Haverford College was recently honored with a visit by Soviet musicologist and music librarian Svetlana Sigida, who is the Director of the Library of the Moscow State Conservatory as well as a specialist in American music. Svetlana was in the United States for September to visit music libraries and do research. On Friday, September 15th, we were fortunate to be included in Svetlana's travels on her way to New York and Boston.

# LIBRARY     N   E   W   S   L   E   T   T   E   R

Svetlana's association with the Moscow State Conservatory spans the last three decades. It was there that she completed both her undergraduate and graduate studies, writing her thesis on "The Life and Work of Aaron Copland" and her dissertation on "Progressive Tendencies in the Music of the United States during the 1930's." She then became a bibliographer, the Assistant Director, Head of the Department of Foreign Relations, and finally Director of the S.I. Taneev Music Research Library. She also serves on the Conservatory faculty. Her publications include many articles on American music and American composers in Soviet encyclopedias as well as journal articles, reviews, and program notes. Svetlana has the honor of being the Vice President of the International Association of Music Librarians.

Our guest was hosted here at Haverford by music faculty member Curt Cacioppo, who met Svetlana while he was in the Soviet Union attending the 3rd International Festival of Contemporary Music. Svetlana spent her morning at Magill Library, first in the Treasure Room with archivist and Russian speaker Diana Franzusoff Peterson and later with reference librarian Margaret Schaus, who helped Svetlana access various databases in quest of citations relating to American opera and American opera composer Marc Blitzstein. In the Soviet Union, finding citations to U.S. materials is very difficult, and Svetlana was pleased to have access here to national databases of books, scores, recordings, and journal articles. After lunch Svetlana came to the Music Library, where, after a brief tour, we settled into more computer searching.

Although it was difficult for Svetlana to break away from her research, the day ended with a reception in the Music Library, giving students, faculty, and librarians a chance to speak with her. She particularly enjoyed speaking with the students studying Russian. It was a pleasure to meet such a fine music librarian, scholar, and, above all, warm and gracious person.

—Donna Fournier

## RESEARCH ADVISORY SERVICE

"What are the economic implications of state lotteries?" "I'm planning to write my senior thesis on Zen Buddhism and Hegel. How do I get started?" "Where can I find information on suicide among slaves in the U.S.?" "I'm studying the evolution of the twentieth-century American literary hero, culminating in the comic book super hero—can you help me find more information?"

These are just a representative few of the Research Advisory questions answered by Magill's reference librarians last year. Now in its third year, the Research Advisory Service provides in-depth reference help for students who request it. The student fills out a form that asks for information on the assignment (length, date due, number and type of sources required), the proposed research topic, sources already consulted, and language proficiency; the form is then passed on to a reference librarian in the appropriate subject speciality. Using the information provided on the form, the librarian develops a search vocabulary for the topic using Library of Congress subject headings and investigates sources at Haverford, Bryn Mawr, Swarthmore, and, if necessary, at other libraries and information sources. The Librarian typically consults library catalogs and both printed and online bibliographies, national catalogs of library holdings, and periodical indexes. For example, for the paper on Zen Buddhism and Hegel, the librarian used the online version of *Philosopher's Index* to find articles indexed under both topics, a much quicker method than using the paper edition of the index to find all the articles about Hegal and then examining each title to see if it were also about Zen.

The librarian then prepares a "plan of attack," a research strategy outlining the results of this investigation. The librarian who worked on the slaves-and-suicide question, for example, prepared a list that included monographs on suicide among blacks; bibliographies on slavery, the black family, suicide in general, and suicide among U.S. minorities; and such indexes as *America: History and Life* and *Sociological Abstracts*. The librarian will have made an appointment to meet the student, and when the student comes in he/she and the librarian discuss the topic, including the advisability of refining and reshaping or changing it, review the research strategy, and look at representative entries in abstracts and indexes. The librarian often demonstrates the use of online bibliographic networks 'like OCLC and PennLIN, as well as local CD-ROM databases, and explains interlibrary loan procedures.

Because the student meets with the librarian in a relaxed, private setting, he/she is often more likely than would be the case at the Reference Desk to think about additional problems or aspects of the topic. At the same time the librarian has the opportunity to get to know the student better and to understand the problems students typically encounter while doing research—information that serves to improve Magill's library instruction program, other library services, and collections. The rapport that develops through Research Advisory appointments often leads to ongoing research relationships because the librarian, knowing the student's interests, can follow up with new books or articles that have just become available.

The Research Advisory Service supplements regular walk-in Reference Desk service in that questions go to a librarian with expertise in a particular subject area; in addition, librarians have more time than is sometimes available at the Reference Desk to identify and

# LIBRARY

N    E    W    S    L    E    T    T    E    R

locate pertinent resources. The Library publicizes this service with forms sent to every junior and senior at mid-semester, during library instruction sessions for individual classes, and by word of mouth among students. Judging by the number of satisfied "repeat customers," it has proved to be a popular and valuable service.

—Kathy Knox

## FACULTY BOOK TALKS

This fall the Library inaugurates an occasional series of "Faculty Book Talks." As new books by the Haverford faculty become part of the Library's collections, the writer will be invited to come to the Library to talk informally about the book. The talks will be advertised on campus and in *Founders Bell*. The first talk in the series, with two or three more to follow this academic year, will be Michael Sells on his *Desert Tracings: Six Classic Arabian Odes* (Wesleyan University Press, 1989) at 4:30 p.m. on Thursday, October 26, in the Philips Wing. The second, tentatively scheduled for late November or early December, will be Julia Epstein on *The Iron Pen: Francis Burney and the Politics of Women's History* (University of Wisconsin, 1989).

## NEW STAFF MEMBERS

As has been the *Newsletter's* custom, we want to let you know about two new members of the Library staff. As the last issue was going to press in the spring, Rosemary McAndrew accepted the position of Circulation Services Supervisor in Magill, in which capacity she is responsible for all Loan Desk and stack maintenance functions. She holds her undergraduate degree from and pursued graduate studies at Johns Hopkins, where she worked for several years in the Eisenhower Library as a Circulation Assistant, Head of Circulation, Reserve Room Librarian, and Librarian for the Undergraduate Library. Prior to coming to Haverford, she had also worked for the Women's Resource Center in Scranton, the Elizabeth Blackwell Health Center in Philadelphia, the Philadelphia office of State Representative Babette Josephs, and the University of Oregon Bookstore.

Donna Fournier became the College's new Music Librarian the first of September. She holds her undergraduate degree in music and mathematics from Connecticut College and her M.L.S. from Southern Connecticut State University. Prior to Haverford, she had been Library Assistant in charge of the Music Library at Connecticut College and, subsequently, in the Yale University Music Library, had worked as an archivist and as a cataloger on a larger, grant-funded retrospective conversion project. She is a cellist and viola da gambist and has taught both instruments. As a professional musician she has played the cello in symphonic and chamber groups and has played the gamba as a soloist as well as in ensembles.

# LIBRARY

N    E    W    S    L    E    T    T    E    R

PUBLISHED BY THE LIBRARY OF HAVERFORD COLLEGE<br>
Haverford, PA 19041 (215) 896-1175

# *The UR Librarian*

## University of Richmond Libraries
## University of Richmond

Format: folder

Size: 8 1/2 by 11"

Color: buff

Number of pages: 5 - 10

Frequency: quarterly

Annual cost: over $1,000

Number of copies: 500-1,000

Audience: faculty, staff, and administration

Editorial responsibility: editorial board; professional librarians

Desktop software: no

# THE UR LIBRARIAN

# New Library Wing To Be Dedicated

During this year's National Library Week, the University Libraries have special cause for celebration. We will gather on April 13 with the University community and friends to rededicate the new and renovated library facilities that support the heart of our academic mission.

National Library Week was initiated 31 years ago by publishers and librarians. It remains the only national promotion program to increase use and support of libraries. This year's celebration has been designated for the week of April 9-15 with the theme

*JOHN TYSON*

"Ask a Professional. Ask a Librarian." The special week mobilizes prominent citizens and librarians at the national and local levels to focus public and media attention on libraries, through workshops and promotional materials. In honor of this year's occasion, University President Richard Morrill has proclaimed the week of April 9-15 as "Library Week" at the University of Richmond.

We all can justifiably take great pride in our expanded and renovated central library with its distinctive and beautiful exterior which maintains the Collegiate Gothic style of the campus. However, the rededication ceremony celebrates more than a building and its impressive architecture. What is most important is what this building says about the University and what it means for the future. The renovation project has produced an enlarged facility that meets the University's present needs and will provide flexibility for the future.

Adding to an existing campus landmark building is a difficult challenge for any architect, particularly when the building is the campus library used by thousands of students, faculty, and community patrons each year. The architectural firm of Marcellus Wright Cox & Smith met the challenge. In spite of many structural barriers, they were able to put together a building which functions very well. We are grateful also to the Board of Trustees, the University administra-

tion, the physical plant staff, the construction workers, and everyone else whose vision and hard work came together to make our "new" library a reality.

As postscript, I am pleased to report two recent major developments. First, the Center for Research Libraries Board of Directors has unanimously elected our library to associate membership. The Center is a membership organization with holdings of nearly five million items of rarely-held research materials that will supplement our local collection. Our election to membership is testimony to the strength of our library. The second development is that the Board of Trustees recently approved approximately one-half million dollars in funding to purchase an automated library system. It is conceivable that when students return in the fall, an automated circulation system will be in place. Eventually all campus libraries will be linked with a computerized library system. Both developments will greatly improve the library staff's ability to meet the increasingly sophisticated information needs of this academic community. ∎

*John C. Tyson*

*—John Tyson*
*University Librarian*

1

2

3

5

4

2

1. *Interior view of the library in Jeter Hall located on the old campus. Note the "black walnut dust-proof bookcases, the latest in library design" in the 1880s.*
2. *Even the 1914 "new library in Ryland Hall soon became crowded."*
3. *Boatwright Memorial Library in its original (1955) form. The entrance, in the tower, faced Richmond Hall.*
4. *Boatwright Library with the 1976 wing. The new entrance faced the lake.*
5. *Boatwright Library today.*

# University of Richmond Libraries: A History

In the collection of the Virginia Baptist Historical Society are two small leatherbound volumes, a Greek New Testament and a concordance, which carry the inscription, "Edw. Baptist, Dunlora 1830." Edward Baptist used these books and others in his personal collection to teach young ministerial students in a private academy he operated, with the blessings of the Virginia Baptist Education Society. Traditionally, the University of Richmond has reached back to Dunlora Academy for its earliest roots; therefore, these volumes mark the beginnings of the library. In 1832, when the Virginia Baptist Seminary, another of the University's roots, was established, funds were raised for "a judicious selection of books as well as a supply of maps and a pair of globes."

The Richmond College catalog of 1843 states that "students would have access to the library by the payment of one dollar per annum." As early as the 1850s the two campus literary societies were forming libraries under their own control and soliciting donations of books. A library directory of 1859 describes the Richmond College collection as containing "1,200 volumes, a few maps, and about 40 diagrams for illustrating natural philosophy." At the time, the library occupied a room, 12 by 18 feet, and was open once a week for half an hour.

This library fell victim to the Civil War in 1861. The students left for battle; the college building, Columbia, was used as a Confederate hospital; and in 1865, after the fall of Richmond, Federal troops were housed in the building. A Union officer carried away the library collection, supposedly for its protection, but only about 70 volumes were ever recovered.

Impoverished themselves at the end of the war, Virginia Baptists soon rallied to aid the school with donations and fund-raising. The college made a glorious comeback. In 1874 a new main building, Jeter Memorial Hall, included "a spacious and elegant apartment" on the "principal floor" for the library. This new space opened with 10,000 books, including 2,000 transferred from the literary societies. The collection grew steadily; there were 20,000 volumes in the library by the time the college moved to the West End in 1914.

In the early years students were appointed to serve in the capacity of librarians. In 1883 Charles Hill Ryland, treasurer of the college, also was designated librarian and curator of the museum. The man who looked after the money also looked after the books!

By 1905 the young college president, Frederic Boatwright, was appealing for funds for the library, declaring that "$50,000 would be but a modest endowment." The endowment undergirded the college library, but in 1911 Librarian Ryland described the income as "slender" and rejoiced that the Trustees "cheer us" with $500 from the general funds.

Upon Charles Ryland's death in 1914, his daughter, Marion Garnett Ryland, became his successor as librarian. She began keeping the library open two hours at night, "a new departure [which] has worked well." She directed the move to Ryland Hall, a multipurpose academic building on the new campus. The second-floor facility, designed after an English university library, was 104 by 30 feet, with a magnificent 24-foot-high vaulted ceiling.

In 1914 the library even began a branch, the Westhampton College Reading Room. It started with several hundred books from the main library placed in the dean's office, and by the next year it had quarters of its own in the tower of North Court. After being displaced during World War I, the room was re-established on campus, and by 1920 had its own librarian, Elizabeth Gaines.

In that same year Miss Ryland already was pleading for more space for the library. "Our library has outgrown the accommodations," she wrote. "We cannot shelve our books or seat students unless we have more room." She called for use of the classrooms in Ryland Hall.

Marion Garnett Ryland was the model of a professional librarian. She kept abreast of changes in library techniques and made large accomplishments with small appropriations. President Boatwright noted, "Because she loved both the reader and the book, she caught the first hint of a freshman's perplexity." Her assistant was Lucy Temple Throckmorton, who upon Miss Ryland's death in 1927 became "acting librarian." She carried that title until a successor was appointed upon her retirement in 1955.

Lucy Throckmorton was more than an "acting" librarian. She was the single driving force behind the library mission and she maintained a steady promotion for adequate space.

By the 1930s the library's growth had necessitated the use of classrooms, literary society halls, and faculty offices. An attempt in 1936 to raise money for a new library building was defeated by economic depression and world war. Miss Throckmorton again in 1943 pleaded with the president to launch a campaign. "I believe it is imperative to raise money now," she reasoned, "as it is likely to be much more difficult after the war with heavier taxes and perhaps less income." She proposed that the building be named for a prominent person, suggesting Charles Hill Ryland, Ellen Glasgow, James Branch Cabell, Douglas Southall Freeman and Edward Baptist.

In 1944 earlier plans for an imposing new library building above the lake were

continued on page 7

3

# Memories of UR Libraries Past

*RAY FRANTZ*

**Ray Frantz** *was University Librarian from 1955 to 1960. He is now the University of Virginia's director of libraries.*

"This was my first job. I have always felt a proprietary interest in the University of Richmond Library, since I helped in designing the interior of the new library in 1955 and also in planning for a book budget to support the immediate needs of the faculty and students. I say 'helped' because I was fortunate to join such people as Josephine Nunnally, Kathleen and Dorothy Francis, and Nita Robinson who knew the territory and could keep the new director from following a false conviction into oblivion. . . . A beginning library director could not have had a better professional experience than to join the University of Richmond in 1955 when a new building was going up and when the case for an increased book budget could be made. I recall being visited in 1957 by a director from another university library who looked around the campus, saw what we were doing, and said, 'You will never be happier.' And in many ways that was true." ▪

**Josephine Nunnally,** *a 1931 graduate of Westhampton College, came back as a librarian in 1938. Now retired, she served as Acting University Librarian between 1960 and 1967.*

"I remember the old library in Ryland Hall very well. I worked there until the new building was opened in 1955. We used to freeze to death in Ryland Hall. There was almost no heat in the library, although theoretically the heat was supposed to come up from the basement. I remember that I always had to wear a wool dress in winter." ▪

*JOSEPHINE NUNNALLY*

**Hannah Coker,** *Music Librarian, Emerita, was graduated from Westhampton College in 1923. She remembers the University's libraries from her student days. (not pictured)*

"It was quite a business hiking over there [to Ryland Hall] whenever we wanted a book. I imagine there was quite a lot of courting went on in that library . . . . We had the Westhampton Reading Room when I was in school. It was in North Court, in the classroom section under the archway. That was nice and convenient. A lot of our class assignments were made to books in that Reading Room. Our faculty in history or English would bring books over when they wanted us to use them. We didn't just go across the lake every day." ▪

4

**Dennis Robison** *was library director between 1974 and 1985. He is now University Librarian at James Madison University.*

"The memory that comes to mind first when I remember the UR libraries is the [1976] move. Everything had to be moved out of the old building and into the new wing before renovation. We had only three weeks to do it and no money, so everyone on the staff helped. Charlie Crowder, a student assistant, actually planned the move within Boatwright, and also took care of the integration of the business collection into the main library. Charlie and a few other hearty folks rented the largest Ryder rental truck we could find and moved the Business Library from the Business School to Boatwright.

They so overloaded the truck that when they were backing it up to the rear entrance of the new addition the drive shaft was bent like a bow and the brakes wouldn't hold! Fortunately, one of the construction people saw what was about to happen and quickly slipped some two-by-fours under the rear wheels. We almost had the truck literally in the cataloging department. Still, we made it in plenty of time to open for summer school." ∎

*DENNIS ROBISON*

**Kathleen Francis** *was a librarian at the University from 1947 to 1985. She worked in two buildings, under five different library administrations. (not pictured)*

"In Ryland Hall it was dark. The more bookcases they added, the darker it got. Eventually it got so that we had books shelved behind books on the same shelf.... When we moved into the new building [in 1955] we really had a lot more space. But the elevator in that building used to sound like it was running by itself. We used to close between 5 and 7, and nights when I worked I would stay after 5 in the building by myself. I just about jumped out of my skin when that elevator would start up. My sister used to say it was the ghost of Dr. Boatwright riding the elevator." ∎

*ARDIE KELLY*

**Ardie Kelly** *retired recently from the position of Librarian at the Mariner's Museum in Newport News. He was University Librarian at Richmond, 1967-1974.*

"The Friends of the Library were started in my time. Jean Wright [then Professor of French] approached me about it. She was very keen on the library. We got together and thought of other people. Evelyn Boatwright Lynch [Frederic Boatwright's daughter] was the first president, and the Peples were involved from the beginning, especially Dr. Peple [Emeritus Professor of English]. One thing that impressed me was the involvement of alumni in the library — how much they used and supported it." ∎

5

# The Dedicatory Volume

*The Book of Kells* is considered one of the finest, most extraordinary works of book art in existence. Although we know all too little about where and when *Kells* was created, we do know quite a bit about how it has been treated during the roughly 1200 years of its existence. Most modern opinion says that it was made at the monastary on Iona, one of the Inner Hebrides of Scotland, somewhere around 800 A.D. Because of Viking raids, it was soon moved to Kells, a monastary in inland Ireland founded by Saint Columba, also the founder of Iona. It remained there until the 1650s when it was threatened by the presence in Kells of Cromwell's troops. At that time it was moved to Trinity College Library, Dublin, and has been there since--one of the great treasures of the Western World.

Now there is a facsimile, made as accurately as a combination of state-of-the-art photography, computer technology, and meticulous human eyes and hands can produce. The new volume has been made as exactly like the old as it can be. The University of Richmond is fortunate to have generous friends such as The Friends of the Library and The Chapel Guild, who, along with a donor who wishes to remain anonymous, donated the funds to purchase this magnificent volume. ▪

*—James Duckworth*

# Frederic W. Boatwright
## 1868-1951

Boatwright Memorial Library is named for Frederic W. Boatwright. Dr. Boatwright was connected with the University of Richmond for 68 years as a student, as president, and finally as chancellor. In 1894, when at 27 he became president of Richmond College, the school had 183 students, nine professors, and 13 acres and $500,000 in resources. When he retired in 1945, the University of Richmond consisted of six divisions, more than 3,000 students and 100 faculty members. The campus had grown to occupy 300 acres and held more than $7 million in assets. The former president long appreciated libraries. He once remarked: "The library is the most vital building in a university . . . the laboratory where every student and every teacher does his work. The educational value of an institution will rise or fall as its library is strong or weak." ▪

*6*

# Boatwright Library Collections

The first catalog of the Virginia Baptist Seminary (a forerunner of the University of Richmond) stated that it was "deemed necessary to spend" $1,000 for the purchase of books. One hundred fifty-six years later, the 1988-89 allocation for Boatwright Library books is over $261,000 and the collection contains more than 400,000 cataloged volumes as well as material in diverse formats such as compact discs and microforms.

Since its inception the library has experienced the ravages of fire and war, but has grown in spite of these disasters. Over the span of years, and concurrent with institutional funding, gifts of personal libraries and book collections have been a significant part of that growth.

Outstanding gifts following the college's reopening in 1866 after the Civil War mark the true beginnings of the present collections. These included 2,597 volumes from Rev. E. J. Owen; 2,000 volumes from the Mu Sigma Rho and Philologian Literary Societies; gifts from the private collections of Rev. J. B. Thomas, Rev. J. B. Jeter, and Dr. W. E. Hatcher. Many of these early gifts are now located in the Rare Book Room.

Later significant gifts from private libraries have given the collection depth in several areas: classics, modern foreign languages, philosophy, religion, history, British and American literature.

Interesting and unique gifts now in the Rare Book Room and Special Collections include over 500 Confederate imprints from the estate of Charles Meredith, law school class of 1871; finely tooled leather facsimile editions of 19th century fiction and original serial publications of some of Charles Dickens' works given by Regina V. G. Millhiser; Westhampton Professor Caroline Lutz's puppet books and journals; the "Mother Goose" collection given by the niece of Miss Helen Monsell,

a former registrar; the Mark Lutz Collection of First Editions of British and American Literature; and a manuscript, books and papers of Carl Van Vechten, noted American writer and critic and close friend of Mark Lutz.

Very recent gifts have included a facsimile edition of The Gutenberg Bible, given by the Friends of Boatwright Memorial Library, and a collection of 20th century autographed fiction donated by the family of William Dew Gresham, a former Boatwright librarian.

The public papers of two former members of the United States House of Representatives from Virginia, Congressman Watkins M. Abbitt from the 4th District and Congressman David Satterfield from the 3rd District are housed in Boatwright Library.

In 1976, the University's Business School Library became a part of the Boatwright Collections. Now known as the Business Information Center, its reference collection consists of more than 6,000 items with specialized resources in general business, finance, accounting, marketing, public relations, and personnel administration.

The University of Richmond was one of the first undergraduate institutions in the nation to establish a full media resources center in 1975. The Learning Resources Center became a part of Boatwright Library in 1976. Its collections in film, video cassettes, audio cassettes, slides, spoken records, filmstrips and kits have grown to more than 17,000 items with strong subject emphasis in the arts, modern European languages, history, British and American literature, the social sciences, education, the natural sciences, health and physical education.

The Virginia Baptist Historical Society, an independent agency of the Baptist General Association of Virginia,

occupies one wing of the Library. The Society is responsible for the administration of the University Archives, which comprise more than 1400 cubic feet of materials relating to female education in the South, College Presidential papers, records and reports of trustees, faculty, administration, and students. Here the development of the University of Richmond is documented from the 1830s to the present. ■

*—Kate DuVal and James Gwin*

continued from page 3

revived. They called for a large tower and "a massive Gothic entrance." The library would have capacity for 300,000 volumes, with costs projected at $400,000 plus $100,000 for book endowments.

The Baptists of Virginia became the focus for fund-raising, and Miss Throckmorton's idea of naming the building after a prominent individual took hold. The long-time president himself was the choice. Costs soared until the original goal of $500,000 was only about half of the needed amount.

When the cornerstone was placed in January, 1955, President Modlin placed in the copper box a copy of the *Alumni Bulletin*, a university catalog, coins and "contemporary objects." Also on hand was a new librarian, Ray W. Frantz, Jr., a recent graduate of the University of Illinois.

Personnel changes were infrequent in the Boatwright Memorial Library, among both librarians and support personnel. Ray Frantz resigned in 1960 to become a librarian at Ohio State University. Josephine Nunnally served as acting librarian until a successor was named. Ardie L. Kelly became librarian in 1967, and guided the beginnings of a new addition. When he resigned in 1974, he

continued on page 8

7

# The Rededication of Boatwright Memorial Library
## Schedule of Events
## April 13-15, 1989

**THURSDAY, APRIL 13, 1989**

| | |
|---|---|
| 2 p.m. | **Lecture** – "The 21st Century: Future Trends in Academic Librarianship" by Dr. Joseph A. Boisse, University Librarian, University of California - Santa Barbara, and President of the Association of College and Research Libraries, Billikopf Learning Resources Center, Adams Auditorium |
| 3:30 p.m. | **Rededication Ceremony** Boatwright Memorial Library (In case of rain, ceremony will be held in Cannon Memorial Chapel) |
| 4:30 p.m. | **Open House and Reception** Music:  String Quartet Tours:  Conducted by Library Faculty and Staff Exhibits: History of the University of Richmond Libraries *Book of Kells* Display and Video Presentation *Gutenberg Bible* Display Lobby, Boatwright Memorial Library |
| 6:30 p.m. | **Friends of Boatwright Memorial Library Annual Meeting and Dinner** Multipurpose Room, Tyler Haynes Commons Keynote Speaker: William Roselle, University Librarian, University of Wisconsin - Milwaukee |

**FRIDAY, APRIL 14, 1989**

| | |
|---|---|
| 8:00 a.m.-<br>9:00 p.m. | **Exhibits:** Lobby, Boatwright Memorial Library |
| Noon-<br>3:00 p.m. | **Library Tours** |
| 6:00 p.m.-<br>9:00 p.m. | **Friends of Boatwright Memorial Library Annual Book Sale,** Boatwright Library, New Addition, Basement Level (members only) |

**SATURDAY, APRIL 15, 1989**

| | |
|---|---|
| 8:00 a.m.-<br>9:00 p.m. | **Exhibits** Lobby, Boatwright Memorial Library |
| 9:00 a.m.-<br>5:00 p.m. | **Friends of Boatwright Memorial Library Annual Book Sale,** Boatwright Library, New Addition, Basement Level (open to general public) |

*continued from page 7*

was replaced by Dennis E. Robison, who completed the building project and introduced computerized cataloging into the library.

By the late 1960s it had become obvious that "growing pains" again were felt by the library. A space needs study in March, 1972 called for a new addition of some 77,000 square feet to allow for more public and book space. The plans were cut to a facility of about 53,500 square feet with about half allocated to house a projected future collection of 500,000 volumes. The addition would increase the library to a total of 90,000 square feet. Renovation of the existing space provided for a small auditorium, faculty carrels, and seminar rooms. A Learning Resources Center was included for production and distribution of media. The School of Business Library and Westhampton Reading Room were brought into the facilities.

Also in the 1970s, two branch libraries were added to the system. The Science Library became part of the university

library system in 1974-1975, and in the next year the Music Library became a branch library.

In 1985 Dennis Robison resigned. James E. Gwin, head of technical services, served as interim librarian until the appointment in 1986 of John Tyson, formerly an assistant library director at Northern Illinois University.

In 1987 construction began on a four-story, 48,000-square-foot addition to the Boatwright Memorial Library as well as renovation of the existing library. The $5 million addition extended the library along the lakeside and provided more space for the Business Information Center and for the reference and government documents collections. Renovation of existing space made more room for the Learning Resources Center, faculty carrels, a new Rare Book Room and the University Archives. ∎

*–Fred Anderson*
*Executive Director,*
*Virginia Baptist Historical Society*

*[Since 1982 Anderson has managed the University Archives. He used archival materials for this article, as well as a 1954 history of the library written by Josephine Nunnally.]*

---

**The UR Librarian** is the official newsletter of the University of Richmond Libraries (Boatwright Memorial Library, Science Library, Music Library).

**Editors:** Bonlyn Hall,
        Lucretia McCulley

**Photos By:** Larry Snedden and
        Fred Anderson

*Correspondence should be addressed to:*
        **The UR Librarian**
        Boatwright Memorial Library
        University of Richmond
        Richmond, Virginia 23173

*8*

# Nameplates

# LIBRARY - FRIENDS NEWS

**ABILENE CHRISTIAN UNIVERSITY**
*Newsletter for ACU Faculty
and Friends of the ACU Library*

By **MARSHA HARPER**
Director of Brown Library

## GIFTS ENABLE GROWTH

Friends and donors! What would we do without them? Although the university supplies funds to meet basic needs, it is from the graciousness of our donors that the library receives the "extras" which are needed for real growth. During the past fiscal year, the ACU Library has received some unusually generous gifts of money, materials, and services.

Cash gifts to the library during the year totaled $13,654. Pride of place for the largest single gift goes to the Lubbock ACU Boosters Club. A check for $7,000 was received from this group, through FACUL, shortly after Lectureship. The money will be used to replace and augment our microform equipment. Since over half the library's total holdings is in micro format (micro-film, -fiche, -print, ultrafiche, etc.), it is essential that equipment in good working order be available to make use of them. Six thousand dollars will be spent to acquire a second reader-printer for both film and fiche, another film reader, two fiche readers, and a special reader for ultrafiche. The remaining $1,000 will be used to fund student searches of the DIALOG computer databases for quick access to journal citations in all subject fields. Both purchases will accomplish the goal of the Lubbock Booster Club to serve students directly; that, of course, harmonizes well with the long-standing goals of the library.

*Marsha Harper, Library Director*

Another significant cash gift was made by **Willa B. Patterson** to fund the design and construction of a case for the Waynai Bible. Of the other gifts, $6,880 of current and accumulated donations was earmarked for memorials and will be used to purchase materials. Gifts made for library equipment and accumulated funds given for no special purpose are all to be used this year to buy $8,902 worth of equipment. Cassette players and head-phones, CD-ROM players, enhancements for the acquisitions and bookkeeping computers, and a cassette duplicator are among the items we will be able to buy. With no budgeted funds for equipment this past year, the gift

*(See **Harper**, page 10)*

*Library Newsletter & Recent Acquisitions*

CONNECTICUT COLLEGE · CHARLES E. SHAIN LIBRARY · GREER MUSIC LIBRARY

Volume 1, no. 5                                        Spring, 1988

### Videocassette/Videodisc Collection

A beginning has been made on a library collection of video materials which will support the educational program of the College. Over 125 tapes and a few discs have been cataloged this year. We will continue to add to the collection as funds permit and as gifts are received, in both Shain and Greer libraries, and we welcome your recommendations for titles to be acquired. Eventually we expect to have the major Public Television series such as The Story of English, but these must await special funding. Send your requests to Peter Berris, Box: Library.

A list of video holdings will be compiled and made available this summer and will be updated from time to time. Meanwhile, many titles now appear in the card catalog and the new CTW online catalog. If you type in "Shoah" on a catalog terminal, for example, it will tell you that we own this notable production (jointly acquired last year with the Department of History) and that its location is "Circulation Desk." Videocassettes and discs may be borrowed by faculty, students and staff only and are due back at 4:00 p.m. the next day. Only one item may be borrowed at a time and it may be reserved by speaking with Mrs. Evento or Mrs. Chambers.

Videocassettes may be watched at the viewing units located in the Microforms Reading Area. Headphones are available at the Reserve Desk. Some 40 or 50 videocassettes are on course reserve again this semester and students wishing to view these are given priority in the use of the equipment. A (very) small room on the second floor will accomodate a group of up to four persons, or five if they are close friends, who wish to watch a tape together. Groups may arrange to view a videocassettes (including their own) in the George Haines Room by calling Mrs. Astrauckas at Ext. 7622.

Brian Rogers

# TITLE PAGE

## RIPON COLLEGE LIBRARY NEWSLETTER

November 1989

## $10,000 BEQUEST

The library has received an unexpected bequest of $10,000 for the purchase of books. In a year that the library has not been able to increase its book budget, this gift comes at a very opportune time. Guidelines for its use have been established by the librarians; primarily it will be used to purchase books which support new or neglected curricular areas. Some reference works will also be purchased; the new Oxford English Dictionary is one purchase made from bequest funds.

## ERIC AND GPO ON CD-ROM

CD-ROM products are the wave of the future for libraries, and Ripon's library has taken the plunge by subscribing to two of these data bases: one in education called ERIC and the other for U.S. government publications. These computer based indexes which can be used by students and faculty members provide multiple searching features and increase access to information in these areas. The first year's subscription to the ERIC database was purchased with funds from a gift to the Education Department.

## VIDEO RESOURCES

Recently one of the librarians was stopped on the sidewalk and asked about the library's video collection. The library does not have a video collection, but what we do have is a list of the videos purchased with college funds and housed in various departmental offices. This list is kept at the circulation desk and is available to anyone interested in determining what videos are on campus. Very shortly the library will be sending department chairs a request to update the video resources list.

## GLASER MEMORIAL FUND

The Glaser memorial fund is a bequest of John Glaser, former professor of history. It is to be used to purchase biographies for the library. Every January a small committee gathers to review submissions and to make decisions about which biographies to purchase. Faculty

# Trinity College Library
## Newsletter

*Published for Students, Faculty, and Library Associates*

Vol. 24, #4

**Fall 1989**

|  | **Trinity Library** | **Watkinson Library** |
|---|---|---|
| Monday-Thursday | 8:30am - 1:00am | 8:30am - 4:30pm |
| Tuesday & Thursday |  | 7:00pm - 10:00pm |
| Friday | 8:30am - Midnight | 8:30am - 4:30pm |
| Saturday | 9:30am - Midnight | 9:30am - 4:30pm |
| Sunday | 9:30am - 1:00am | CLOSED |

**Christmas Vacation**

| | | |
|---|---|---|
| December 21 & 22 | 8:30am - 4:30pm | 8:30am - 4:30pm |
| December 23 - 26 | CLOSED | CLOSED |
| December 27 - 29 | 8:30am - 4:30pm | 8:30am - 4:30pm |
| December 30 - Jan. 2 | CLOSED | CLOSED |
| January 3 - 5 | 8:30am - 4:30pm | 8:30am - 4:30pm |
| January 6 & 7 | CLOSED | CLOSED |
| January 8 - 12 | 8:30am - 4:30pm | 8:30am - 4:30pm |
| January 13 & 14 | CLOSED | CLOSED |
| January 15 & 16 | 8:30am - 4:30pm | 8:30am - 4:30pm |
| January 17 | Resume Regular Hours | Resume Regular Hours |

# IMPRESSIONS

## Newsletter of the Schmidt Library
## York College of Pennsylvania

## Be Quiet. . . . . Please

Schmidt Library Staff have recently launched a "Quiet Campaign," in order to halt an often serious noise problem caused by talkative Library users. Persons who talk in the Library while socializing, or while working together on assignments, have made conditions impossible for others who wish to study. As a result, signs have been posted which designate special "Quiet Study Areas."

> This is a
> QUIET
> study area.

These areas consist of the East and West Wings (first and second floors), and Periodicals Services in the Lower Level. Library Staff have been making extra efforts to approach persons who cause a disruption, to notify those persons that their behavior is inappropriate, and to request that they leave if such behavior is continued. In the event of a Library user refusing to cooperate, campus security personnel will be summoned.

Thus far, the majority of Library patrons appear to be respecting the attempts to maintain an appropriate library environment. Such support is greatly appreciated by Schmidt Library Staff, who will continue to do what they can to "keep the peace." The public is reminded, though, that staff cannot be in all Quiet Study Areas at the same time. Therefore, patrons are urged, when necessary, to promptly notify a Staff person of disrup-

tions which arise, and to consider taking the initiative in requesting a stop to inappropriate noise.

Bill Markley

## 27 New Titles Added
## in Fourth Year of
## Periodicals Project

The third annual review of departmental requests for new periodicals titles was completed by Susan Campbell, Cheryl Kirby, and Sue McMillan. After evaluating requests from eight of the ten departments, 27 new subscriptions were entered at an approximate cost of $1,500. This brings to 88 the number of new titles added to the collection since the Periodicals Project began three years ago.

The success of our project has spread. It is interesting to note that it has served as a model for Susquehanna University. Librarians there have in turn shared the process with Lafayette College.

Continuing efforts in Periodicals Services will include microform conversion, collection development and retention policies, and examination of closed stacks in an automated environment.

Susan Campbell

Volume V, Number 2      November, 1989      Susan M. Campbell, Editor

# Graphics

EUGENIA FULLER ATWOOD LIBRARY, BEAVER COLLEGE

# from the LIBRARY

VOLUME VI, NUMBER 1     THE ATWOOD LIBRARY - BEAVER COLLEGE     SEPTEMBER, 1989

WELCOME

**COME SAY HELLO TO OUR NEW LIBRARY STAFF MEMBERS!**

Welcome to our new Serials Assistant, Rani Nadarajah.

Rani received her bachelor's degree Magna cum laude in Computer Science and Chemistry from Jersey City State College, New Jersey. She also has a diploma in Library Sciences from Sri Lanka.

Rani is very appreciative of her welcome to the library and is looking forward to becoming involved with activities on the campus.

Welcome also to Mary McGinty who has joined our staff in the Interlibrary Loan Department.

Mary is a former Beaver employee who took time off to raise a family. She lives in Harboro with her husband, Bob, and daughters, Maria and Elizabeth.

> T'ai Chi is the ancient Chinese way to health and longevity. Gentle, deliberate movements refresh the body, revitalize the spirit and clear the mind. T'ai Chi improves book circulation, strengthens the cardiovascular system, massages the internal organs and supplies the entire organism with life energy.—*Princeton (N.J.) Packet.*
>
> Attention, librarians!

CAMPUS DIRECTORY

○ Needs new plumbing
□ Needs new roof
△ Needs elevator
▭ Needs new windows

## CIRCULATION OF VIDEOTAPES

Now you can watch a library videotape in your own space! The circulation of library videotapes has been changed from Use in Library Only to 24-Hour Loan. After 24 hours, fines are charged for late returns at the Reserve book rate. Borrowers must also assume responsibility for possible damage or loss. The library has a variety of tapes: the graduate colloquia series, opera tapes such as DON GIOVANNI and SAMSON AND DALILA, a series on the civil rights movement, foreign language and physical therapy tapes, Nova series tapes, a teaching strategies series, and travel tapes on the British Isles, to a list a few. Check us out and learn by viewing. Note: As before, a photo I.D. <u>must</u> be <u>presented</u> before signing out this material.

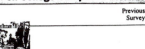

## What They're Reading on College Campuses

|  |  | Previous Survey |
|---|---|---|
| 1. | **Yukon Ho!** by Bill Watterson | 1 |
| 2. | **Wildlife Preserves**, by Gary Larson | 5 |
| 3. | **Chaos**, by James Gleick | 7 |
| 4. | **The Cardinal of the Kremlin,** by Tom Clancy | — |
| 5. | **The Mummy**, by Anne Rice | 4 |
| 6. | **Codependent No More,** by Melody Beattie | — |
| 7. | **The Dark Tower: The Gunslinger,** by Stephen King | — |
| 8. | **The Silence of the Lambs,** by Thomas Harris | — |
| 9. | **The Dance of Anger,** by Harriet Goldhor Lerner | — |
| 10. | **Zoya,** by Danielle Steel | — |

The Chronicle's list of best-selling books was compiled from information supplied by stores serving the following campuses: American U., Baylor U., Bucknell U., Carleton College, Carnegie Mellon U., Case Western Reserve U., Central Michigan U., Dartmouth College, Idaho State U., Indiana U., Kent State U., Lawrence U., Lehigh U., Mankato State U., Montana State U., New York U., Pennsylvania State U., Portland State U., Princeton U., San Francisco State U., Stanford U., Syracuse U., Tarrant County Junior College, Tulane U., U. of California at San Diego, U. of Hawaii, U. of Iowa, U. of Maryland-Baltimore County, U. of Missouri at Columbia, U. of Nebraska at Lincoln, U. of New Orleans, U. of Notre Dame, U. of Pittsburgh, U. of Puget Sound, U. of Washington, U. of Wisconsin at Madison, Vanderbilt U., and Xavier U. (Ohio). Reports covered sales of hardcover and paperback trade books in July.

## NEW BOOKS IN WOMEN'S STUDIES

Dr. Edith Gross, Sociology Department, has spearheaded an effort to fill in the gaps of the library's holdings in the area of Women's Studies. Approximately, sixty new titles have been received. Others are on order. These new acquisitions include BATTERED WOMEN by Lenore Walker; BLACK WOMEN IN WHITE AMERICA, Gerda Lerner; COMPARABLE WORTH AND WAGE DISCRIMINATION, Helen Remick; CONGRESSIONAL WOMEN, I.N. Gertzog; GENDER GAP, Bella Abzug; JUDGE, LAWYER, VICTIM, THEIF: WOMEN, GENER ROLES AND CRIMINAL JUSTICE, Nicole Rafter; LANGUAGE, GENDER, AND SOCIETY, Barrie Thorne; NEW CATHOLIC WOMEN, Mary Weaver; PROFESSIONAL WOMEN AND MINORITIES, Betty Vetter; NONSEXIST RESEARCH METHOD, Magrit Eichler; RETHINKING THE FAMILY, B. Thorne, Editor; WHY WE LOST THE E.R.A., Jane Mansbrige; WOMEN'S WORK AND CHCANO FAMILIES, Patric Zavella. Keep abreast of recent research and contemporary trends by consulting these new additions.

## FRIENDS DINNER

The Friends of Atwood Library are planning another holiday dinner. This one features Peggy Anderson author of the best selling novel, Nurse. Among Ms. Anderson's many credits are two other books, Children's Hospital and The Daughters: an Unconventional Look at America's Fan Club! the D.A.R. and articles in such magazines as Ms., Family Circle, the New York Times Magazine, and Philadelphia Magazine. Ms. Anderson is formerly from Chicago but now makes her home in Philadelphia. She will speak at the holiday dinner on the topic of "One Writer's Experience."

The dinner promises to be a lot of fun. The date is December 10th, the time is 6:00 p.m. and the place is Grey Towers Castle. Cost of the dinner is a modest $35.00 per person. Anyone wishing to be a sponsor of this fundraiser may send a check for $75.00 (includes one ticket) to Friends of Atwood Library, Beaver College, Glenside, P.A. 19038. Patrons may send $125.00, (two tickets) and Benefactors may give $250.00 (four tickets). The proceeds from the dinner will go towards the purchase of new moveable shelving for the library, so even if you can't make the dinner, you may wish to send in a holdiay gift for the library. Hope to see you there!

Here´s the answer to our last newsletter puzzle.

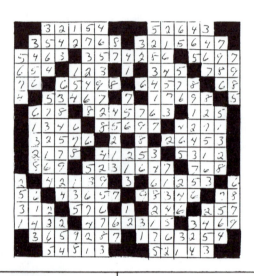

# Across Town, or ''Across the Universe''

Whether you need a book on Halley's Comet or the Beatles, your library can get it for you, even if it's not part of its collection.

Ask your librarian about Interlibrary Loan. You'll find that there's more to the library than the eye can see.

COME IN TO THE ATWOOD LIBRARY !

## NEW SHAKESPEAREAN CRITICISM ACQUISTIONS

At the request of Dr. Hugh Grady, English Department, the library´s collection of Shakespearean Criticism has been given a much needed update and boost. Carolyn Dearnaley, Library Director, has authorized the purchase of several new works. Sample titles received are as follows: THE WOMAN´S PART: FEMINIST CRITICISM OF SHAKESPEARE, RADICAL TRAGEDY: RELIGION, IDEOLOGY AND POWER IN THE DRAMA OF SHAKESPEARE AND HIS CONTEMPORARIES, BROKEN NUPTIALS IN SHAKESPEARE´S PLAYS, and THE PLACE OF THE STAGE: LICENSE, PLAY, AND POWER IN RENAISSANCE ENGLAND. Other titles have been received and complement the Gale Research Series of Shakespearean Criticism a reference series also owned by the library.

## TRY OUR NEW NEWSLETTER PUZZLE

Remember the old hink pink game? One person gives a definition, the other person supplies the answer, to which is a pair of words that rhyme. For example, a fruit thief is a melon felon, or a sign for a horse ranch might be a stable label. Well, a cannon canon is a law governing the use of large guns or a bargain on iron might be a steel steal. Other times they are multiple meanings of the same word form: a fair fair might be defined as a mediocre exposition, or a person who sells property boundary markers on the black market might be called a fence fence.

1.   The correct answer as to the identity of a mystery liquid in a chemistry class (hinkity hinkity)

2.   A quick diet involving complete abstention (hink hink)

3.   A serious tomb (hink hink)

4.   Someone who monitors the output of a factory producing a game played a lot on park benches (hinky hinky)

5.   Someone who monitors the people in 5 (hinky hinky hinky)

6.   A stand-in below water machine (hink hink)

7.   A more sunburned leather processer (hinky hinky)

8.   A sixth tire for a car (hink hink)

9.   A period of time when everyone's into motor bikes (hinky hinky)

10.   A high quality group of students (hink hink)

11.   A contest to determine which company makes the best fire lighters (hink hink)

12.   A farm animal stricken with laryngitis (hink hink)

GOOD LUCK !   LOOK FOR THE ANSWERS IN THE NEXT NEWSLETTER.

FARLEY MEMORIAL LIBRARY, GEORGIAN COURT COLLEGE

# LibraryLines

## Georgian Court College

Vol. III, No. 1

September 1989

LAKEWOOD, N. J. 08701

FARLEY MEMORIAL LIBRARY

## WHERE ARE THE BOOKS?

If you have had difficulty in locating certain books, especially those in the Dewey classifications 370-372 and 001-099, we remind you that we are in the process of converting the library collections over to the Library of Congress Classification. Since new catalog cards take longer to file than it takes to process the books, you may still encounter old cards in the catalog after the book has been reclassified. If this happens, please consult the librarian at the Reference Desk, who will be happy to help you determine the new call number and locate the book you need.

At the present time, books with the Library of Congress classifications "A" and "B" are shelved on the upper level, to the right of the door leading to the rear wing. Classifications "C" through "Z" are in the main floor Reading Room. Materials may be moved during the year as the reclassification progresses, so watch for signs and be sure to ask at the Reference Desk if you have any difficulties.

## LIBRARY HOURS

Regular schedule during the academic year:

| | |
|---|---|
| Monday-Thursday | 8:30 am-10 pm |
| Friday | 8:30 am-4:30 pm |
| Saturday | 10 am - 4 pm |
| Sunday | 1 pm - 5 pm |

Hours will vary on holidays and school vacations. A complete schedule of library hours and holidays is available in the lobby information rack.

## IN THE NEWS

Recent events in China have piqued Americans' interest in that country. For those members of the Georgian Court community who would like to read something about the life and culture of China, we suggest the following titles recently added to the library:

Chen, Nien. _Life and death in Shanghai_. DS778.7.C445 1987

Gao, Yuan. _Born red: a chronicle of the cultural revolution_. DS778.7.G36 1987

Macleod, Roderick. China, Inc.: how to do business with the Chinese. HD58.6.M33 1988

Spence, Jonathan D. _The death of the woman Wang_. HQ1767.S63 1979

Theroux, Paul. _Riding the iron rooster: by train through China_. DS712.T446 1988

Yu, Leslie Tseng-tseng. _Chinese watercolor painting: the four seasons_. ND2068.Y8 1988

# FROM THE DIRECTOR

Hello again! Welcome back to campus. For various reasons, we did not print any issues of LibraryLines last year, so with this one we'll try to bring you up to date on activities at Farley Memorial Library.

What have we accomplished over the past few months?

*Most of the Reference Collection and nearly all of the circulating collection in the area of education has been reclassified and converted to machine-readable form in preparation for a future automated library system.

*The part of the Reference collection in Library of Congress classifications "Q" through "V" has been moved to the upper level because we ran out of space in the main floor Reference area.

*Additional shelves in the Reading Room to accommodate more new books and reclassified materials were installed and are nearly full already!

*The Instructional Media Center (IMC) has been relocated from the Arts & Sciences Building to the library's upper level.

*The New York Times Index, the microfilm holdings of the New York Times, and two microfilm reader/printers are now located in the Reading Room.

*A computerized acquisitions program has been implemented, providing faster and more efficient ordering of library materials.

*We purchased an additional microfiche reader/printer, making a total of four machines available for using this type of material. Another reader/printer was converted from microfiche to microfilm use, making two available.

## AUDIOVISUAL DEPARTMENT

The AV Department is alive and growing in both the Library and the A & S! Colleen Lynch (our AV Technician) will be happy to help you with the local production of AV materials, including custom made transparencies and slides. Beginning in September 1989, she will also handle all AV rentals for you. This service has been requested by many faculty members, so we hope you will use it. Guidelines and request forms will be available in the AV Office (A & S 132).

The AV materials collection in the library is in the process of being updated and expanded. Barbara Herbert may be contacting your department for assistance in "weeding" the collection of those materials which are outdated. An inventory of AV materials was begun this summer, so we would appreciate the return all AV materials to the library.

New circulation procedures for AV materials have been established. The circulation period is one week (one renewal may be permitted if there are no other requests for the item). Fines for overdue AV materials are $ 2.00 per day.

## COLLECTION DEVELOPMENT

One of the goals of the library's long-range plan is to strengthen the book collection. Since the collection is measured not only by the number of volumes, but also by its relevance to the curriculum and to the research interests of the faculty and students, we welcome the participation of faculty members in the selection process.

Laura Gewissler, Collection Development Librarian, encourages faculty members to send her copies of their class syllabi and reading lists for checking against the library's holdings. Requests for new or classic older titles are also welcome. For more information or to obtain book request forms, call Laura at ext. 423.

## RESEARCH SERVICES FOR FACULTY

### DATABASE SEARCHING

Through the Dialog Search Service, the Reference Department has access to several hundred online databases listing journal articles, documents and other information sources. These databases cover many subject fields, including education (ERIC), business (ABI/Inform), psychology (PsychINFO), history (Historical Abstracts, and biology (BIOSIS). A bibliography on virtually any topic can be produced for you very rapidly. For more information, contact Mary Meola, ext. 422.

### INTERLIBRARY LOAN

Books and journal articles not in the library's collection can be obtained through interlibrary loan. The computerized OCLC network enables library staff to locate needed items and place the requests electronically. Our membership in the Central Jersey Regional Library Network connects us with most libraries in the state via daily delivery service, thus reducing the time you must wait for interlibrary loans. For more information, contact Mary Meola or Michele Donovan, ext. 422.

### PRINCETON ACCESS CARD

The library has purchased an access card for the Princeton University Library, which may be used by any member of the GCC faculty. This card allows the holder to conduct research at Firestone Library, but does not permit the borrowing of library materials. The card is available from the office of the Director of Library Services and may be reserved in advance. For more information, contact Barbara Hutchinson, ext. 421.

1989—YEAR OF THE LIBRARIAN
"Ask a professional.
Ask your librarian."

TELEPHONE DIRECTORY

Acquisitions    ext. 423

    Laura Gewissler
    Marie Monto

Audiovisual    ext. 379

    Colleen Lynch

Cataloging    ext. 424

    Reya Maxymuk
    Bill Goertz
    Donna Capuano
    Elvene Clements
    Edith Muller
    Sheila Steinman
    Sister Evelyn

Circulation    ext. 419

    Mary Ellen McClinch
    Connie Williscroft
    Mary Winn

Director's Office    ext. 421

    Barbara Hutchinson
    Loretta Donato

IMC    ext. 479

    Barbara Herbert

Periodicals    ext. 420

    Marie Respass
    Bonnie Otto

Reference    ext. 422

    Mary Meola
    Michele Donovan

VIDEO ACQUISITIONS

During the past year the library has expanded its audiovisual collection to include videocassettes. All are in VHS format and may be borrowed for a period of one week for classroom or home use. Videos may also be previewed in the library.

Recent acquisitions include:

A-V BL304.C36  The power of myth  (6 cassettes)
A-V DP402.T74S67 1986  Spirit of the Alcazar
A-V LB3013.C42  1988  Classroom management
A-V LB3013.C5  1978  Classroom management techniques
A-V M1045.B7Y6 1985  Young person's guide to the orchestra
A-V M1500.B625C38  Bizet's Carmen
A-V M2000.H3M53 1983  Messiah
A-V ML410.I94C42 1987  Charles Ives: a good dissonance like a man
A-V ML3760.D57 1987  Discovering the music of Africa
A-V N2030.C46 1983  A tour of the Louvre
A-V N2940.V345 1983  A tour of the Vatican Museums
A-V N3450.P72 1983  A tour of the Prado
A-V N5630.L5 1988  Light of the gods
A-V NB237.N43N4 1977  Nevelson
A-V NX652.W6E4 1982  The eighteenth century woman
A-V PN1997.M5835 1985  Modern times
A-V PN1997.N595 1984  El norte

For more information about the video collection, or to suggest titles for purchase, please contact Barbara Herbert, ext. 479.

# Indiana University at Kokomo

# LRC NOTES

## Learning Resource Center

Volume 2, Number 1    Spring 1989

## CARS - COMPUTER ASSISTED REFERENCE SERVICES

### CD-ROM

C D - R O M (compact disk - read only memory) disks are easily mistaken for audio CD's. In fact, the only difference between a CD labeled *Der Ring des Nibelungen* and one labeled *ERIC* is that the former encodes music while the latter encodes type. The information on either disk is read by reflected laser light and decoded into digital bits before coming to us as either music to our ears, or letters to our eyes.

The capacity of a CD-ROM is enormous. Each disk can hold the equivalent of over 1500 floppies (360k) or over 27 hard disks (20MB). This is equal to about 270,000 pages of text, which would weigh 2800 pounds and take up over 110 feet of shelf space.

A multitude of data, from the entire maintenance manual for a Boeing 747 to magazine indexes, are published in CD-ROM. Clients of the LRC have access to business and education information through this technology.

*ERIC* (a database which comprises *Current Index to Journals in Education* and *Resources in Education*) and *Business Periodicals Index* are entering their ninth month of service to individuals at the LRC. Over 130 faculty, students, and other users know the wealth of information available at their fingertips through CD-ROM. (We think the number is much higher, but not all users sign in when they use the computers).

Diane Bever introduced CD-ROM technology to IUK in the fall of 1988. In December she scheduled demonstrations for interested faculty, administrators, and staff. Ms. Bever and Christian Poehlmann continue to demonstrate this technology in the classroom by means of a liquid crystal display projection unit. To arrange for one of these demonstrations, contact Mr. Poehlmann at extension 265.

Indiana University at Kokomo

Vol. 2, No. 1, Spring 1989

# LRC NOTES
Learning Resource Center

## NurseSearch

*NurseSearch* is a nursing literature database stored on the hard disk of an IBM personal computer located in the CARS area of the LRC.

IUK nursing students can look forward this summer to an even better computer search system. NurseSearch has ceased publication as of 1988. It will be replaced by CINAHL (Cumulative Index to Nursing and Allied Health Literature) in its CD-ROM version. CINAHL on CD-ROM provides coverage for a greater number of both years and journal titles than NurseSearch. Search enhancements also include the ability to search several years of the index at one session rather than one year at a time as required by NurseSearch.

## CONGRATULATIONS

Congratulations to LRC Director Dick Ardrey on his 25th year of service to IUK. Mr. Ardrey was presented with a gold watch at a dinner held in his honor on January 14.

A portrait of Mr. Ardrey was presented to the university and is now on display in the main building.

Mr. Ardrey began his career with Indiana University on the Bloomington campus in 1962. In 1965, at the same time the main building at IUK was being completed, Mr. Ardrey moved to the Kokomo campus.

Congratulations also go to Head of Reference Diane Bever who has been at IUK 10 years as of February.

## GOVERNMENT PUBLICATIONS

### Shelflist

A computerized shelf-list for the government documents collection has been developed by Christian Poehlmann, the Government Publications Librarian. This shelflist will be stored in machine readable format on the hard disk of an IBM PS/2.

A shelflist will enable the librarians to immediately determine if the LRC holds a particular government publication as well as determine where that document is housed. This innovation should encourage further use of the collection.

### Featured Government Publications

How many times have you been looking for detailed information on a foreign country and not wanted to

Indiana University at Kokomo

Vol. 2, No. 1, Spring 1989

# LRC NOTES
Learning Resource Center

check-out twenty books? The government documents collection may be able to fulfill that need. The area handbook's are a continuing series prepared by the Library of Congress under the Country Studies - Area Handbook Program. Most texts in the series deal with a particular foreign country, describing and analyzing its political, economic, social, and national security systems and institutions. The interrelationships of these systems, and the ways they are shaped by cultural factors, are also examined. Each study is written by an interdisciplinary team of social scientists.

## WELCOME BACK

The LRC welcomes back Jeff Coon as a part-time reference librarian. Jeff is originally from Kokomo and most recently from Texas.

## LETTER FROM THE EDITOR

This issue of the *LRC NOTES* is the first under my editorial control. It was produced using Wordperfect version 5.0 and an HP Laserjet series II printer.

Any comments, suggestions, and material for inclusion in later issues would be greatly appreciated. Such material may be sent to me in care of the Learning Resource Center at Indiana University at Kokomo.

*Christian Poehlmann, Editor*

## REFERENCE BOOK SPOTLIGHT

This edition of the *LRC Notes* puts the reference book spotlight on the second edition of the *Oxford English Dictionary*, otherwise known as the *OED2*.

The *OED2* has a long and rich history. The first edition of this dictionary was published in 1933 in a twelve-volume set. This first *OED* was a reprint of the ten-volume *New English Dictionary*, itself a product of parts originally printed and distributed between 1884 and 1928. The *OED2* contains the complete text of this first edition.

The *OED2* also contains the complete text of the *Supplement to the Oxford English Dictionary* which was published between 1972 and 1986; this supplanted the previous *Supplement* which was published concomitantly to the first edition. The *OED2* also contains approximately five thousand new words, or senses of existing words, which have gained currency since the germane edition of the *Supplement* was published.

INDIANA UNIVERSITY AT KOKOMO LEARNING RESOURCE CENTER, INDIANA UNIVERSITY AT KOKOMO

Indiana University at Kokomo                    Vol. 2, No. 1, Spring 1989

# LRC  NOTES
Learning Resource Center

The raison d'etre of the second edition is the amalgamation of the 252,259 entries of the first twelve volumes, the 69,372 entries of the four volume *Supplement*, and the approximately 5,000 new words and definitions previously undocumented in the *OED* and its supplements.

The new edition of the *Oxford English Dictionary* contains about 290,500 main entries. This is about 15 per cent more than in the first edition. The text has grown from around 44 million words to around 59 million; an increase of about 34 per cent. If printed characters were counted, the total would round out to about 350 million. A total of 616,500 word forms are contained in this edition. There are 137,000 pronunciations, 249,300 etymologies, 557,000 cross-references, and 2,412,400 illustrative quotations.

# ANNOUNCING

## NEW PERIODICAL TITLES

*Critical Inquiry*

*Novel: A Forum on Fiction*

*Scholarly Inquiry for Nursing Practice*

*Accounting Today*

*Wisconsin Small Business Forum*

*Poets and Writers Magazine*

# STAFF

Director:
Richard Ardrey

Head of Reference:
Diane Bever

Reference and
Government Publications Librarian:
Christian Poehlmann

Part-Time Reference Librarian:
Jeff Coon

Secretary and Government Publications Assistant:
Debbie Hachet

Media Specialist:
Terri Hellmann

ILL/Circulation Supervisor:
Kim Maxwell

Acquisitions/Serials Assistant:
Janine Stanley

A-V Media Technician:
Walt Baker

SUMMER HOURS

MAY 8-AUGUST 10

Mon. - Thurs.: 8:30am - 8:30pm

Friday: 8:30am - 5:00pm

Saturday: 12:00 noon - 5:00pm

Sunday: CLOSED  MAY 27 - 29,
JUNE 24, JULY 1 - 4:  CLOSED

UTICA COLLEGE

# Bibliophile

## Frank E. Gannett Memorial Library
Vol. 1 No. 2     **NEWSLETTER**     July 1988
\* \* \* \* \* \* \* \* \* \* \* \* \* \* \* \* \* \* \* \* \* \* \* \* \* \* \* \*

Although it is often said that one should not mix business and pleasure. This issue of the Bibliophile flagrantly violates that rule, but then again so does the Gannett Library. In summer, the library provides a home away from home to an incredibly diverse clientele.

Some, of course, are students busy with coursework. Others explore for the joy of satisfying their intellectual curiosity, and yet others consider the library a place to relax. This Bibliophile is an attempt to meet the needs of all these users.

In it you will find both informative stories about new developments at the library and media center, as well as handy tips to make your research easier. This newsletter, however, presents an exciting expose on harassment of librarians by the FBI, and just in time for summer, it features a list of recent fiction and biography -- meaty works, perfect to devour in your leisure time. So no matter why you use the library, this issue of the Bibliophile has something inside it for you.    (E.H. Kramer)

\* \* \* \* \* \* \* \* FBI in the Stacks \* \* \* \* \* \* \* \* \*

A recent article in The Nation (April 9, 1988) outlines the FBI's "Library Awareness Program"--an attempt by the FBI to induce librarians to report on reading habits of foreigners or "suspected spies." Several university, special, and public libraries have been contacted. Closer to home, Village Police in Whitesboro recently asked the Dunham Public Library to release circulation records of certain individuals who might have checked out books on Satanism.
In both these instances, the librarians refused to release the information. Were you surprised by their response? We weren't. According to the American Library Association's Code of Ethics: (Continued PAGE 6)...

## SUMMER READING

The Library now has a leisure reading shelf containing
fiction, biography, and travel books. A selected list follows:

## FICTION

Beattie, Ann.
Where You'll Find Me and
other stories. Collier
Books, 1987. Short stories
which previously appeared in
the New Yorker, Vanity Fair
and Esquire. Stories of
upper-middle-class people of
the 80's. PS3552/E177W4/1987

Godwin, Gail.
A Southern Family. Morrow,
1987. Clare Campion, a
successful NYC novelist,
visits her family in North
Carolina. The violent death
of her brother during the
visit causes repercussions
for each family member.
PS3557/O315S6/1987

Gordimer, Nadine.
A Sport of Nature: a novel.
Knopf, 1987. Hillela, a white
South African, grows to
maturity in the land of
apartheid. At the conclusion,
she is the wife of the head
of state of a different
African country, and attends
the proclamation of the new
(liberated) South Africa.
PR9369.3/G6S67/1987

Gordon, Mary.
Temporary Shelter: short
stories. Random House, 1987.
The title story concerns an
adolescent boy whose mother
works as a live-in house-
keeper. Other stories tell of
Irish immigrants in America.
PS3557/O669T4/1987

Keillor, Garrison.
Leaving Home. Viking, 1987.
A collection of thirty-six
short stories taken from
everyday events in ordinary
people's lives in the author's
imaginary hometown, "Lake
Woebegon, Minnesota."
Monologues featured on
Keillor's Prairie Home
Companion radio show.
PS3561/E3755/L43/1987

Morrison, Toni.
Beloved. Knopf, 1987. Former
slave, Sethe, is haunted by
the spirit of "Beloved," the
baby daughter she killed to
save from slavery. The baby's
ghost is driven from the
mother's home, only to be
replaced by a strange young
woman. PS3563/O8749/B4/1987

Ozick, Cynthia.
The Messiah of Stockholm.
Knopf, 1987. Lars Andemening,
a Polish refugee, is obsessed
with publishing the manuscript
of Bruno Schulz' last novel,
The Messiah. Illusion and
reality blur in this dream-
like novel. PS3565/Z5M4/1987

Wolfe, Tom.
Bonfire of the Vanities.
Farrar, 1987. Outrageous
satire of NYC mores. While
driving with his mistress in a
Mercedes, Wall Street bond
trader, Sherman McCoy, makes a
wrong turn off the highway and
meets disaster in the South
Bronx. PS3573/O526B6/1987

## BIOGRAPHY

Ellmann, Richard.
<u>Oscar Wilde</u>. Knopf, 1988.
Portrait of the Victorian
"most tragic figure."
his early years in
Dublin, his education at
Oxford, through lecture
tours in America, the man
who created "The Importance
of Being Earnest" comes to
life before proceeding to a
tragic death at forty-six.
PR5823/E38/1988

Hanna, S.S.
<u>The Gypsy Scholar: a</u>
<u>Writer's Comic Search for a</u>
<u>Publisher</u>. Iowa State Univ.
Press, 1987. "All college
professors would love to
publish as often as animals
mate on the nature programs
of PBS television," states
the foreword to this
humorous picture of education
in the small college. The
author tells of seeking a
position teaching English in
a glutted market, while
trying to find a publisher
for his manuscript, "The
Gypsy Scholar."
PN155/H27/1987

Hurston, Zora Neale.
<u>Dust Tracks on a Road: an</u>
<u>Autobiography</u>. 2d ed. Univ.
of Illinois Press, 1984.
The author's account of her
rise from childhood poverty
in the South to become one of
the great figures in
twentieth century American
literature and Afro-American
culture.
PS3515/U789/Z465/1984

(E. Pattengill)

Miller,        Arthur.
<u>Timebends: a Life</u>. Grove
Press, 1987. Miller's Age's
autobiography proceeds From
nonchronologically from early
Brooklyn    childhood    to
McCarthy's witch hunts to
marriage to Marilyn Monroe.
Miller also describes his
early struggles in the
theater.
PS3525/I5156/2477/1987

Murray,        Pauli.
<u>Song in a Weary Throat: an</u>
<u>American pilgrimage</u>. Harper,
1987. Involved in social
reform movements from the
1930's to the 1980's, Murray
describes her childhood in
the South, her participation
in the civil rights movement,
and her career as a lawyer,
writer and poet who
eventually became an
Episcopal      priest.
E185.97/M95A3/1987

Schwerin,        Doris.
<u>Diary of a Pigeon Watcher</u>.
Paragon   House,   1987.
Recovering from cancer
surgery, the author
identifies with a family of
pigeons nesting on her window
ledge. Ordinary events become
transformed into universal
themes as she remembers her
own  family's  history.
PS3569/C5697/Z464/1987

Washington, Mary Helen.
<u>Invented Lives: narratives of</u>
<u>black women 1860-1960</u>. Anchor
Press, 1987. Selections from
eight writers, including
Gwendolyn Brooks, Ann Petry,
and Zora Neale Hurston.
Excerpts from Harriet Jacobs'
<u>Incidents in the Life of a</u>
<u>Slave Girl</u>. PS647/A35I58/1987

## What's All the Excitement About?

The circ. staff is very excited about computerized circulation. Our new system is both speedy and versatile. With it we instantly check on availability of materials and can reserve them for you as well.

Under automation, students and staff can borrow books for twenty-eight days with one renewal, while the book circulation period for faculty is sixty days with up to a year's worth of renewals allowed in most cases. (All items are still subject to recall.)

We are currently re-evaluating our circulation policy to better meet the college community's needs. We will of course announce any policy changes in the Bibliophile.

Each week the Mid-York Library System prepares our overdue notices. Fines are as follows: books,10¢/day with a seven day grace period; records 10¢/day with no grace period; and journals and class reserves 50¢/day. After seventy-six days, the computer classifies a book as "lost" and charges a replacement fee.

Unfortunately, not all library materials are part of automated circulation. This is in part because some items remain to be inventoried and more seriously, because some materials taken out prior to January 19, 1988 are still at large. Faculty and staff, please return these wayward books, journals, and records NOW! Remember automation works for you, and your cooperation can make it work even better!

(M. Fox)

## Making Mathematics Easier

To a student taking introductory math, the library is more than just a quiet place to do homework; for the Gannett Library's reference shelves now contain several works geared toward students in beginning courses. Although these can not replace a professor's help or assistance at the UC Math Resource Center, we do offer answers to at least some basic mathematical questions.

For those taking calculus or applying it to physics and/or engineering, the CRC Handbook of Chemistry and Physics(Ref QD65 H3) lists integrals inside both its front and back covers.

If you need an explanation for a particular type of problem, Problem Solvers stand at the ready. Currently only The Calculus Problem Solver(Ref QA303 C35) is available, but problem solvers for algebra (both elementary and intermediate) and geometry (plane, analytic, etc...) are on order and due to arrive shortly. (E.H. Kramer)

## Serials Notes

The serials collection is presently undergoing extensive evaluation and reorganization. Due to the escalating costs of subscriptions, and the need for new titles, it is necessary that each journal be carefully examined for its relevancy to our curriculum and interest to our academic community

To date, we have cancelled only those subscriptions deemed by the faculty as no longer useful, and we have ordered recommended replacements. We continue to elicit the advice of the college community.

We bring attention to the need for libraries to network with each other to assure complete access to all significant journals. Our participation in SUNY-OCLC national and state serials system provides ready electronic access to most titles holdings, as well as a highly effective order and delivery system. While interlibrary loan capabilities in no way decrease our need for a comprehensive collection, they do provide the vehicle for acquisition of the more rare and exceptional items via a national database which includes Great Britain.

In an effort to consolidate our serials collection, we are in the process of replacing missing issues so that we can bind complete volumes. Again, evaluation of an individual serial determines the cost-effectiveness of replacement. We would appreciate the return of any journal issues or bound volumes which may be on your book shelves across the campus. In addition to needing the item to complete our holdings, all items are needed to complete inventory for our online catalog.
(P.        Burchard)

## Try the Vertical File

The next time you need up-to-date or specialized information for a research project, why not try the vertical file in addition to books and magazines?

The vertical file, is a collection of pamphlets and reprints of articles on a wide variety of topics. It is housed in several large grey cabinets near the new book shelves, and the reader services office.

The file emphasizes recent and controversial issues such as acid rain, AIDS, and computer applications. Vertical file pamphlets on scientific subjects, often deliver sophisticated information in a form which the general public can understand, and best of all, vertical file material circulates for three days.
(E.H.        Kramer)

"Librarians must protect each user's right to privacy with respect to information sought or received, and materials consulted, borrowed or acquired."

New York State law provides further support. (CPLR s. 4509): "Records related to the circulation of library materials... shall be confidential and shall not be disclosed except [through] subpoena [or] court order." More recent legislation adds computer searches, reference requests, and title searches to the previously protected circulation records.

Be assured that faculty may not request to view circulation records of their students. Nor are interlibrary loan requests public information. In keeping with each individual's right to privacy, the library will refuse to honor demands to release such information.
(E.      Pattengill)

### Africa and Africans through Art

Continuing this summer is a display of African art and sculpture on loan from several Utica College faculty and staff. The exhibit was arranged by Stacy Shelnut, a UC senior. Take a walk behind the center stairway to view such objects as an Ashanti fertility doll, wood and ivory carved elephants, a chief's ceremonial sword, wooden masks, and a hair pick from the Malawi tribe.
(E. Pattengill)

### More Handouts for You

The Gannett Library's handout collection has grown considerably since the last Bibliophile issue. Tipsheets and bibliographies are now available on such coursework related topics as pharmacology, occupational therapy, and bioethics. A handout on chemistry for those with a nonscience background is a special addition to this collection and there is also a horticulture reading list of interest to both serious and armchair gardeners alike.

These handouts are of course located near the reference desk, and like the Bibliophile, they hopefully offer something for everyone.
(E.H.      Kramer)

## Coming This Fall

Mark your calendars for the weekend of September 30. Utica College will host a Polish festival. The celebration kicks off with the formal opening of a Polish art exhibit at the Edith Barrett Art Gallery.

Events scheduled for Saturday October 1, include the film, The Polish Phoenix,

lectures, seminars, dance demonstrations, and Polish folk music.

Continuing throughout October will be a display of Polish books donated by Tom Lawrence, to the Utica College Library.

---

WHO WE ARE

The Bibliophile, the official Gannett library newsletter is published every semester. Its staff include:

Editor -- Painan Wu

Assoc. Editor --
    Elizabeth Pattengill

Graphics -- Terry McMaster

Technical Consultant --
    Eileen Kramer

---

ALSO

---

Guest Columnists

Patricia Burchard
and
Margaret Fox

---

# Style Manuals/Guidelines
# for Guest Editors

## GENERAL INFORMATION

1. **PURPOSE:**  Encourage interest in and support the mission of the library, promote the services of Bertrand Library and its collection, provide schedules and descriptions of upcoming library events designed for the public, interpret library policies for the public, illustrate new equipment and its uses, report on gifts to the library, foster image of the library in the community, note professional activities of librarians, and report on broad information issues.  An issue may contain various topics, or may focus on <u>one</u> theme.

2. **TONE:**  The tone of CONTENTS is dignified without being stiff.  The style is relaxed, without being unduly informal.

3. **AUDIENCE:**  The general reader: focus on members of the Bucknell community, such as Friends of the Library, Administration, Faculty/Staff.  Do not direct to library staff.  It is important to remember to avoid library jargon and excessive detail.

4. **FREQUENCY:**  Issues are printed quarterly:  September, December, March, and May.  Special issues are possible. (The first issue was published February, 1985.)

5. **LENGTH:**  Although the normal issue is four pages, the newsletter can be expanded to six pages by inserting a sheet into the folio for special issues.

6. **ARTICLES:**  Articles should be of interest to a general (i.e., non-librarian) audience.  In particular, articles should report on major library projects and acquisitions, wide interest information issues, and professional activities of Bucknell librarians.  From time to time, profiles of librarians may be included.  Occasionally an issue will be devoted to one topic, and/or maybe edited by a guest editor (any member of the library staff).

   Articles should be brief and free of library jargon and excessive detail.  A <u>major item should take no more than 3/4 page</u>.  News items should be kept between 1/4 to 1/2 page.

7. **FORMAT:**  Use two column format; columns are 3 1/2" wide. Pre-printed <u>Contents</u> stock available at Administrative Services.

8. **CONVENTIONS:**
   Underlining:  word by word.
   Online:  spell as one word.
   Dormitory:  use residence hall instead.

Capitalization:   Bucknell University's public relations
    capitalizes very few items.   Committee names,
    professional titles, departments, are all typed in
    lower case.   The word "library" is typed in lower
    case except when it appears as part of the phrase
    "Bertrand Library."
Quotation marks:   commas and periods at the end of
    quotes are always enclosed in quotations (e.g.,
    "Love's Labors Lost,").
Database:   spell as one word.
Computer-readable:   as an adjective use a hyphen.
Computer readable:   as a noun requires no hyphen.

9.  **TYPING:**   Articles typed and edited using Microsoft Word.
    Imported into desktop publishing software (Aldus Pagemaker)
    using newsletter template.

10. **PHOTOGRAPHS AND ILLUSTRATIONS:**   Some copyright free woodcuts
    and clip art are available online or in Library Office
    publication files.

    Illustrations and photographs can be reduced at
    Administrative Services as part of the paste-up process.

11. **PASTE-UP, PRINTING, AND MAILING:**   Paste-up, printing, and
    delivery to the mail room is handled by Administrative
    Services in accordance with instructions on the work order
    (see example).   Work orders should be cleared with the
    Assistant to the Director of Library Services before they go
    to the Supervisor of Processing for Administrative Services.
    A minimum of two-week turn around is required.

12. **MAILING LIST:**   The mailing list is maintained by the
    Assistant to the Director of Library Services.   Newsletters
    are distributed via U.S. bulk mail rate or through the on-
    campus delivery service.

**PLANNING AND PREPARATION**

Planning and preparation should begin at least six weeks prior to
the projected publication date.   See formula.

1.  Review list of possible articles, submitted articles, and
    respective authors for issue with the Director of Library
    Services for comments and suggestions.   Revise accordingly.

2.  Ask specific individuals to write articles.   Provide these
    writers with clear specifications (e.g., length, focus,
    deadline).   Request any needed photographs from media
    services (see example).

ELLEN CLARKE BERTRAND LIBRARY, BUCKNELL UNIVERSITY

**CONTENTS:   EDITOR'S MANUAL**
Page 3 of 3

3. Edit articles written by others and write additional
   articles needed for issue.  Submit to the Director of
   Library Services in typed form.  Send copies of articles to
   authors, if requested.

4. Review copy and revise as necessary.  Submit revisions to
   Library Secretary for retyping onto disk.

5. Submit final copy in Newsletter format, including all
   illustrations, to Director of Library Services for final
   approval.

6. Have final copy proofed twice by persons unconnected to
   project.

7. Print final copy to laser printer, using laser paper.
   Prepare dummy, marking all illustrations (page number, crop
   marks).  Be sure to include all captions.

8. Complete work order for Administrative Services (see
   example).  Be sure to note that the editor should see paste-
   ups before printing.

9. The editor makes an appointment with the Supervisor of
   Processing at Administrative Services (8 Marts Hall) to
   deliver all copy and pictures, and to discuss the work
   order.  Submit copy.  Allow ten days for printing and
   delivery to the mail room.

10. Send memo with mailing list to the head of the mail room
    indicating that CONTENTS is coming (see example).

11. Review paste-up, checking for picture captions, placement of
    illustrations, spacing of copy, and correct masthead.
    (Masthead should be numbered according to academic year,
    e.g., Vol. II no. 3, Winter 1987).

12. Six weeks after distribution, all newsletters which have
    been returned for incorrect addresses should be used to
    update mailing lists.  Any mailing label with a long number
    at the top should be sent to University Relations to update
    Friends of the Library list.

12/87;Revised 3/90

2

# B U C K N E L L

## memo

From: Ann de Klerk and
Arlieda Ries

To: Library Staff

Date: June 29, 1988

Subject: Guidelines for Guest
Editors of CONTENTS

### CONTENTS - PURPOSE, TONE AND AUDIENCE:

**Purpose:** Encourage interest in and support of the mission of the library, promote the services of Bertrand Library and its collection, provide schedules and descriptions of upcoming library events designed for the public, interpret library policies for the public, illustrate new equipment and its uses, report on gifts to the library, foster image of the library in the community, note professional activities of librarians, and report on broad information issues. An issue may contain various topics, or may focus on <u>one</u> theme.

**Tone:** The tone of CONTENTS is dignified without being stiff. The style is relaxed, without being unduly informal.

**Audience -** the general reader: focus on members of the Bucknell community, such as Friends of the Library, Administration, Faculty/ Staff. Do not direct to library staff. It is important to remember to avoid library jargon and excessive detail.

**DUTIES OF THE EDITOR:** generate ideas, assign articles, order photos or art work, edit stories, assure that articles have been typed on library office computer disk, write headlines, request comments from the Director, send articles to Public Relations for editing suggestions, place stories and illustrations on page layouts, write up printing instructions, check the final paste-up. See CONTENTS Manual for more detail - re: timing and components.

**ROLE OF THE GUEST EDITOR:** on occasion a member of the library staff, other than the regular editor, may be invited, or may volunteer to act as guest editor of CONTENTS. This will introduce more variety in style, tone, and perspective of CONTENTS while allowing an outlet for creative expression of the librarians and other staff. In general, the guest editor will plan an issue, discuss with editor and library director, solicit and/ or write articles, arrange for illustrations or photographs following the procedures outlined in the CONTENTS manual (in the HANDBOOK).

AdeK/kc

Revised February 27, 1990
**DACUS FOCUS**

**PROPOSED EDITORIAL GUIDELINES TO GO INTO EFFECT JULY 1, 1982**

I.  Mission
    The mission of <u>Dacus Focus</u> shall be:
    A.  To inform the library's clientele about Dacus Library activities, services, resources, policies, and staff.
    B.  To reflect on library trends that will, could, or do impact on Dacus Library.
    C.  To acknowledge and publicize substantive contributions to the library.

II. Audience
    <u>Dacus Focus</u> will be sent to :
    A.  Faculty and administration of Winthrop College.
    B.  Certain campus departments or bodies not having faculty or administrative members, e.g., Career Placement Office, Alumni Office, <u>The Johnsonian</u>, etc.
    C.  Decision-making bodies with influence on the library, i.e., the Board of Trustees, the Board of Visitors.
    D.  All contributors to Forces of Resources (cash contributions), as well as donors of collections or resources deemed significant by Archives or Acquisitions.
    E.  Selected area and regional libraries, library schools, and archives.

III. Inclusion Policies
    A.  Feature articles should be related to one of the following:
        1.  Noteworthy, different, or interesting projects, changes, or achievements in services, policies, or staff library-wide.
        2.  State, regional, or national developments that would impact <u>local</u> library users.
        3.  Special events sponsored by or held at the library.
    B.  Regular features include:
        1.  "The Den of Antiquity"; a column devoted to Archives and Special Collections.
        2.  "Active People"; a column on significant staff activities.
    C.  Items to be used only for filler include:
        1.  "Meet the Staff" or staff change articles.
        2.  Items of local or statewide history taken from archives records.
        3.  Publicity announcements for existing services (and then only if not recently promoted in the newsletter).
        4.  Significant library statistics (used only rarely).

  5. A column dedicated to new reference acquisitions (written in narrative form rather than as a list of books).

  6. A column on new documents (also in narrative form).

 D. Excluded items include:

  1. Donor lists. (These are suitable for separate publication.)

  2. Items of interest only to other library professionals, e.g., meeting reports, which should be published in <u>The South Carolina Librarian</u> or some other vehicle.

  3. Gossip items of in-house interest only.

  4. Complicated procedures that go on behind service activities.

  5. Calendars of events.

  6. Book or journal reviews.

IV. Editorial Procedures

 A. Timetable

  1. Frequency
   <u>Dacus Focus</u> should be published twice a year, in the fall and the spring.

  2. Dates
   Suggested target distribution dates are October 15th and April 15th. The editor is responsible for the final choice of publication dates.

  3. Schedules
   The editor is responsible for setting up a production schedule to meet whatever date has been chosen.

 B. Length

  1. <u>Dacus Focus</u>
   The newsletter itself should not be more than eight letter size pages long. Anything longer than that or in another size should be approved first by the Dean of Library Services.

  2. Articles
   Copy submitted should be a maximum length of 1 1/2 to 2 pages of double--spaced type, the norm being 1 to 1 1/2 pages.

 C. Soliciting Articles

  1. Requesting general contributions
   The editor should route a memo to all library staff alerting them to the opportunity of contributing to <u>Dacus Focus</u>; asking them to notify the editor of their intention to turn in something; and informing them of the deadline to submit copy. The editor is responsible for the final selection of articles, and is under no obligation to use all of the items received.

  2. Requesting news
   At about the same time as the memo is sent out,

the editor should ascertain from the Dean of Library Services, as well as from division and department heads, what noteworthy items they feel should be covered in the newsletter. This step could be done formally or informally, according to the editor's preference.

3. Requesting specific articles
The response to the general appeal for newsletter items may not be sufficient for a complete issue, or no one may submit copy about a certain event or service that the editor would like to feature, and it may become necessary for the editor to approach individuals to request specific articles. It is suggested that this be done (again, formally or informally) soon after the memo mentioned above has been sent and a preliminary response to it has been received. In this way, the copy deadline is the same for every one.

D. Approval
Once the content of the newsletter has been decided, a copy of the edited articles should be submitted to the Dean of Library Services for comment, revisions, and final approval.

E. Mailing list maintenance
1. Routine
With each issue, a statement near the address label should say, "If you no longer wish to receive this publication, check here and return this form to..."
2. Special
Once a year, the mailing list should be reviewed by the editor and other appropriate staff.
Once every two years, address corrections should be requested from the Postal Service.